TIGER'S NEW SWING

TIGER'S NEW SWING

AN ANALYSIS OF TIGER WOODS'S NEW SWING TECHNIQUE

John Andrisani

Foreword by Jim McLean

ST. MARTIN'S PRESS ⚭ NEW YORK

www.stmartins.com

Book design by Gretchen Achilles

ISBN 0-312-35540-8
EAN 978-0-312-35540-1

First Edition: November 2005

10   9   8   7   6   5   4   3   2   1

I dedicate this book to **EARL WOODS, RUDY DURAN, JOHN ANSELMO,** and **BUTCH HARMON**—all of Tiger Woods's former teachers—who each left his indelible mark on Tiger's technique before present coach Hank Haney took on the challenge of helping Tiger build an even more consistent and efficient, powerfully accurate new golf swing.

CONTENTS

1. THE PROCESS   9

To become a powerfully accurate shot maker, you must go through what Tiger Woods calls "The Process" and be willing to make changes to your setup, backswing, and downswing, even if that means choosing a new golf instructor to guide you.

2. SETTING UP FOR POWER AND CONTROL   39

Use Tiger's unique setup position to promote controlled, hard-hit shots.

3. GETTING YOUR BACKSWING BACK ON TRACK   67

To swing back on a unique circular upright plane like Tiger so that you are poised to employ a powerful, on-balanced downswing action, learn and groove this golfing superstar's new body–club positions.

SPECIAL EIGHT-PAGE COLOR INSERT
TIGER'S TURBO-DRIVE SWING: CAUGHT ON CAMERA

following page 78

4. DOWN TIME   89

Correctly timing the downswing is all about coordinating the movement of the body with the movement of the club while generating power centers and maintaining the angle in the right wrist until impact.

5. THERE'S ONLY ROOM FOR IMPROVEMENT   115

In the search for the perfect swing, even a player like Tiger Woods has had to learn from his mistakes and groove good habits through drill work on the practice tee.

ACKNOWLEDGMENTS

The process of writing this book was a lot like learning a new golf swing; it requires patience, persistence, hard work, and a wonderful team behind you.

I'm grateful to literary agent Jake Elwell of the Wieser & Elwell Literary Agency, and to editor Marc Resnick of St. Martin's Press, for believing that it was time Tiger's **new swing** was analyzed, and the secrets I've discovered about his powerful technique shared with some twenty-seven million golfers that play this wonderful game around our country.

I thank photographer Yashiro Tanabe and artist Allen Welkis for their fine work in helping readers visually appreciate Tiger's new swing and, too, compare it to his old swing through wonderfully candid pictures and illustrations.

I deeply appreciate great teacher and good friend Jim McLean, for his technical insights and for writing the foreword, as he did in 1997 when I wrote *The Tiger Woods Way*.

I thank Tiger's former teachers, all of whom have given me their inside advice over the years on things they taught Tiger and even shared some hidden secrets regarding Tiger's masterful swing.

I'm also grateful to golf instructor Hank Haney for the fine work he's done on Tiger's swing, and for proving to critics and struggling amateur players that new changes can work wonders—provided you stick to a plan, stay positive, and practice diligently. Thankfully, Hank's views on the golf swing have remained consistent since I first interviewed him in 1991 and elected him to *Golf Magazine*'s 50 Best Teachers in America list.

Finally, I thank three women for their fine support: civil engineer Deborah Atkinson, for encouraging me to analyze Tiger's swing from various angles to get a true "read" of his unique technique; Lana Mills, a fine pianist, gourmet cook, and painter, whose creative spark and hard work under art mentor Carlo DiNapoli was an inspiration to me when writing this book; and my late mother, Gwendoline Andrisani, whose lifetime perseverance and lasting poetic writings kept me typing early in the morning and late into the night, always making sure to choose the right words in order to relay the right message to golfers.

FOREWORD

All golfers love to hear ideas and opinions on the greats of the game, and no professional golfer commands more interest than Tiger Woods. Tiger has dominated his peer groups since age three and has stood head and shoulders over his competitors during his entire golfing life.

Nobody will ever match Tiger's record of winning three consecutive United States Junior and three straight United States Amateur championships. It will never happen again. Tiger's feat of capturing all four major championships at one time will be hard to duplicate as well. Averaging a shot total of 67.79 per round in 2000—a full one and a half strokes better than the second best player on the PGA tour—is another statistic of Tiger's that blows my mind, and probably yours, too. I could go on and on talking about Tiger's accomplishments, but I will let John Andrisani continue the story in this book and offer his opinions and his research on the Tiger Woods swing saga.

Back in 1997 I wrote the foreword to John's bestselling book, *The Tiger Woods Way: An Analysis of Tiger Woods'*

Power-Swing Technique. For this new book, John has interviewed and talked with many teachers, writers, and professional golfers. I've been just one teacher John has spoken to about the most recent changes Tiger has made in his golf swing.

When I wrote articles for *Golf Magazine,* starting in the early 1990s, John was head instruction editor. I learned quickly that he was a ball of energy and a man with hundreds of ideas. John took an article I researched and wrote for *Golf Magazine* in 1992 and titled it "The X-factor." That title has become a worldwide phrase among golfers talking about power-swing mechanics.

John has hammered home important technical points on Tiger's golf swing, and some stated in this book will be looked upon as controversial. But that's okay. John will back up his story with facts. After all, that's the only way to seek the truth. And, in this case, all of us want to know the truth about Tiger's new swing and how the changes have evolved.

Over the last few years, everyone in the golf community has recognized that Tiger Woods has gone through a major swing change. After an incredible run from 1999 through 2001, when Tiger really distinguished himself in his sport, as only Babe Ruth and Michael Jordan had done in their respective sports, Woods left his golf teacher, Butch Harmon.

That fact that Tiger would massively change the swing that won him (by fifteen strokes) the U.S. Open at Pebble

Beach in 2000 is remarkable. He also won other events by double digits. Yet Tiger has always been willing to take risks to get even better at golf and improve on what he learned from his father, Earl Woods, his mother, Kultida Woods, Rudy Duran, John Anselmo, navy clinical psychologist Jay Brunza, and of course Butch Harmon, who taught Tiger from age 17 to 27 and helped him become the number-one-ranked player in the world—a position he got knocked out of after leaving Butch but that he has now regained once again. In *Tiger's New Swing,* you will learn about the major contributions made by all of the aforementioned individuals and new coach Hank Haney. But first let me set the scene with a couple of Tiger anecdotes.

In 2002, after winning five of six major championships, Tiger began working on making a major swing change. John Andrisani will give you his take on the changes Tiger has made since that time. At first there was a significant drop in Tiger's ball striking. He eliminated his famous "stinger" shot, changed his backswing, and his overall statistics went downhill, most significantly his driving accuracy. Ironically, whereas in the past, every pro golfer would have loved to swing the driver like Tiger, by 2003 that was no longer true. Suddenly, a huge weapon for Tiger Woods was actually hurting his game.

However, during Tiger's down period he never got negative, owing to his incredibly strong mental fortitude and out of his all-world short game. Tiger always insisted that he was "getting close," despite huge evidence to the contrary—his downward trends in PGA Tour statistics—and stayed positive regardless of sportswriters, television analysts, and golf instructors questioning his decision to make drastic changes to his swing. During this two-year period Tiger was magical in staying near the top in almost every tournament. There was (and is) no give-up in Tiger Woods and he remained convinced improvements would come. He battled through more than two years of numerous ugly shots by making fabulous recoveries.

Finally, in 2005 Tiger began to see good results. At Doral, where one of my golf schools is located, I watched Tiger win the Ford Championship, with a score of 24 under par. Tiger also won the Masters in 2005, but it was a couple of months later at the U.S. Open when his power-fade tee shot really started to pay off. In fact, some golf experts, including this book's author, believe that, had Tiger putted better, he would have won that championship instead of finishing second to New Zealander Michael Campbell. Well, in July, things all came together for Tiger during the British Open at St. Andrews, where he drove the ball superbly and sunk enough putts to shoot a score of fourteen under par and win this coveted championship by five strokes. And in August 2005, Tiger hit the ball well enough to nearly win the PGA played at Baltusrol Golf Club in Springfield, New Jersey. Tiger finished in fourth place.

The bottom line: Tiger is so talented that he can make any swing method work. It looks like he has now pretty much figured things out. All Tiger ever cared about was getting better and it appears that he is now finally accomplishing his goals. Time will tell if he will completely revert back to his old form and "Terminator" status on the world golf stage. In the meantime, I can only say that Tiger is the most gifted and talented player I have ever seen. He is also the most exciting player to watch. And I love reading about him, as you obviously do. I hope *Tiger's New Swing* helps you understand how Tiger's technique evolved and that you can apply some of the tips contained in it to your own game.

JIM McLEAN
Doral Golf Resort and Spa
Miami, Florida

TIGER'S NEW SWING

INTRODUCTION

When viewing the painting *The Matador,* the first ever done by Pablo Picasso, at age eight, and then looking at other drawings and watercolors of his mother and father that he created just five years later, I witnessed the work of a child prodigy, thanks to this rare collection of pieces assembled by the Museum of Modern Art in New York City. However, it was only when I learned the degree to which Picasso daringly took chances throughout his long career, rose above scathing criticism at the onset of the Blue Period and Cubist Movement, and continued painting anyway according to his hot-blooded Spanish instincts, that I appreciated his true genius.

Eventually, Picasso's confident attitude and steady creative drive paid off. Proudly, he stood outside his success, and the fame and money that go with it, only caring about self-satisfaction and the legacy of works he would leave behind in museums, marking his greatness.

I feel the same way about Tiger Woods as I do about Picasso, because Tiger has painted shot-making pictures for all to marvel at on golf course canvases around the world.

Tiger has taken creative chances, risen above criticism, and proven over and over again that the innovative changes to his swing, that many golf experts believed he was crazy to make, work and work well. Like Picasso, Tiger is a genius who is proud of his efforts and eager to continue to be creative and improve his "art." Yet, as a former full-time golf instructor and senior instruction editor at *Golf Magazine*, even I wonder to what extreme Tiger will go in his search for swing perfection. After all, his present, virtual flawless technique, developed under new golf coach Hank Haney, won Tiger the Masters and British Open in 2005. And though still being tampered with and tweaked, like paintings by Picasso that he said were never really complete, Tiger's new swing is so technically sound that I find it hard to believe that it can get any better, as you will read about and see for yourself by looking at the wonderful photographs showing Tiger's magical power-driving technique.

I felt a sense of déjà vu when writing this book, which I guess is no surprise, because in 1997 I wrote *The Tiger Woods Way*, in which I analyzed Tiger's power swing.

This time around I will present you and other avid golfers with an analysis of Tiger's *new* driver swing technique, based on what I determined were dramatic changes made to this virtuoso's setup, backswing, and downswing since taking lessons from one of golf's top-ranked teachers, Hank Haney, who is best known for helping PGA Tour player Mark O'Meara win two major championships, the 1998 Masters and 1998 British Open.

I have always admired the golf philosophy and work of Hank Haney, a very patient teacher, who rather than follow a fools-rush-in philosophy, analyzes swing faults, strongly considers the flight plan and trajectory of the ball, thinks logically and sensibly about solutions, then makes calculated changes to the swings used by pros and amateur golfers. I realized Haney was a special breed of teacher way back in 1991, when I first spoke to him after reading his answers to a questionnaire designed by me when I was senior editor of instruction at *Golf Magazine* and was assigned the arduous task of picking the best fifty teachers in America for our publication's prestigious list. Today, judging from the successful overhaul job he's done on the swing of star student Tiger Woods, there are many golf experts that consider him golf's best teacher.

Haney has certainly helped Tiger improve (since Tiger first asked for help from him in March 2004), which is the bottom line mark of a good teacher. However, there are other individuals and golf instructors who helped Tiger establish a strong foundation for Haney to build on.

In *Tiger's New Swing*, I track the evolution of Tiger's powerfully accurate technique, citing important contributions made by Tiger's father Earl Woods, plus professional golf instructors Rudy Duran, John Anselmo, and Butch Harmon. All these individuals deserve credit for helping Tiger evolve into a great golfer. Yet, make no mistake, Hank Haney is the one man who over the last few years has made the most dramatic changes to Tiger's swing.

I believe wholeheartedly that reading *Tiger's New Swing* and understanding what makes this great golfer's technique tick—based on what I learned from observing Tiger, talking to experts, and analyzing the changes made by Haney—will enlighten you. Moreover, once you groove each of Tiger's new setup and swing positions, through diligent practice, the more quickly you will evolve toward hitting the ball better, both in terms of power and accuracy. All you have to do is remain patient, persevere even when you don't see instant results, and stay positive, and I promise you are likely to experience the rewards of revamping your present swing and raising the level of your golf game.

As a prelude to my independent analysis of Tiger's setup and swing, let me provide you with some bullet point highlights of what's so different about Tiger's present technique, compared to his old action.

TIGER'S NEW SETUP

Tiger's body alignment is slightly open to the target line, and he now plays the ball more forward in his stance and tilts his left hip higher than his right. This new address position ultimately enables Tiger to contact the ball on the upswing and hit a highly controlled power-fade shot that, incidentally, is easier to learn how to play than a draw.

(Previously, Tiger set his shoulders open and his feet slightly closed, while playing the ball well in back of his left heel and keeping his hips level. This address position promoted a draw shot that did not carry as far. Furthermore, if Tiger released the club extra-powerfully in the impact area, his draw sometimes turned into a duck hook—a shot that flies well left of target and usually lands in deep rough, among tall trees, or in a water hazard.)

TIGER'S NEW BACKSWING ACTION

Tiger now makes a fuller, upright backswing, marked by a stronger shoulder turn and a less-active hip turn. By limiting hip turn during the backswing, Tiger builds resistance between his upper and lower body and, in turn, creates powerful torque. This power is transferred through the arms and hands, then to the club in the hit zone, so that, once the ball is struck, speed is maximized. Consequently, Tiger hits the ball longer than ever.

(Previously, while taking lessons from Butch Harmon, Tiger cut his backswing back to three-quarter length and did not make as full a turn. This more compact swing helped Tiger improve his distance control with irons. However, unless Tiger's timing was perfect, this shorter action had a negative effect on his driving skills. Tiger's swing was so short and rounded that he often looked compelled to swing down faster. Even for Tiger, who practiced hard, the short swing eventually ended up doing him more harm than good. When you employ a very compact backswing, you lose turning power, find it much more difficult to time the downswing, and thus have trouble consistently returning the club squarely and solidly into the ball at impact. The result: a loss of power and accuracy.)

TIGER'S NEW DOWNSWING ACTION

Tiger now keeps his left shoulder, arm, and club on a circular plane, and his right foot stays on the ground longer. This new downswing action, that's slightly less upright in nature to the backswing action, enhances Tiger's balance, allows him to time the downswing better, deliver the club's face solidly into the ball more easily and consistently, and hit a higher percentage of powerfully accurate drives.

(Previously, Tiger swung the club on more of an exaggerated, tilted plane or angle, so that the club had to travel farther from inside the target line on its way to impact. Tiger's club often became trapped or blocked by his body, so it was natural for him to react by clearing his hips too briskly in order to free himself up, and also flip his right forearm and right hand over his left forearm and left hand in an attempt to square the clubface. The result: a severe hook shot.

Previously, too, Tiger sometimes exaggerated the push action of his right foot. This fault, involving lifting too much of the right shoe off the ground too quickly, hindered Tiger's balance and caused him to hit the ball well right of target.)

Before you begin reading this book that describes the changes in Tiger's setup and swing, access your present technique, then look inside yourself to truly determine if you are willing to sacrifice some playing time with friends for some hard, honest, solitary practice.

Every single time during his golfing life that Tiger decided to switch coaches, he had to be willing to reduce his tournament schedule to learn new setup and swing keys, as well as to devote hours and hours to practicing until a particular movement was drilled into his muscle memory.

The secret to learning to repeat a new and better swing, over and over, involves three words: tempo, timing, and rhythm. Only if your action is synchronized, and flows as smoothly as a concerto by Mozart, will it operate to maximum efficiency. I'm not suggesting that you will not hit any solid shots if your swing is a little out of sync, just that you will hit a lower percentage of quality shots.

A main reason why Tiger left Harmon to work under the tutelage of Hank Haney was to find a swing that allowed him to hit a higher percentage of good drives. But it was also to find a type of action that would allow him to swing at a high speed (tempo), harmoniously coordinate the movement of the club with the movement of the body (timing), and feel as if the entire motion operated effortlessly (rhythm).

In *Tiger's New Swing*, I will present you with what I call "Tiger Tips," based on my analysis of what makes golf's number-one virtuoso's swing work so well. It's up to you, and perhaps your local professional, to select how many of the Tiger-Tips you want to try and incorporate into your existing swing. Tiger's new swing is much easier to learn than any I've ever seen, simply because the plane is more upright and the club stays closer to the target line, from the time it swings back until the time the ball is struck. Therefore, if you can even devote a solid hour of practice time each day for a month, I trust that you will see a noticeable change in your ability to hit the ball longer and straighter, particularly with the driver.

Your journey will begin the second you start reading chapter 1, the purpose of which is to educate you on the process that's involved in learning to improve your driver-swing technique and take control of the golf ball's flight. After that, it's a matter of grooving Tiger's setup and swing secrets, by reading the remaining chapters and studying the instructional photographs. My advice: understand each technical swing change before you make it, visualize yourself employing each new movement, and then devise a realistic practice plan to help you feel the flow of the full motion. Follow these simple guidelines and you will become a stronger and straighter hitter of the golf ball.

JOHN ANDRISANI
Gulfport, Florida

1. THE PROCESS

To become a powerfully accurate shot maker, you must go through what Tiger calls "The Process," and be willing to make changes to your setup, backswing, and downswing, even if that means choosing a new golf instructor to guide you.

T iger Woods calls the search for the perfect swing a process, which is a euphemism for constant experimentation relative to the basics governing the setup, swing, and shot-making technique, extreme practice sessions, and an uncanny ability to somehow stay enthusiastic and even-tempered when swing changes fail to yield immediate, positive, and encouraging results on the golf course.

The French philosopher Jean Paul Sartre explained in *Being and Nothingness,* his existential literary masterpiece, that since childhood humans are obsessed with filling holes, citing cases of boys and girls sticking their fingers in their mouth or making holes in walls then sticking their fingers in the holes to fill them.

Since childhood, Tiger Woods has been obsessed with knocking a little white ball into a four-and-one-quarter-inch hole in the least number of shots, and thanks to the early guidance of Earl Woods, his father and first swing mentor, Tiger learned that the only true shortcut to low scoring is developing a good golf swing—one that is easy to repeat, produces powerfully accurate shots, and performs consistently well under pressure.

There have been many great players who have come to this same realization, most notably Bobby Jones and Jack Nicklaus. But not since Ben Hogan dominated golf in the 1950s, winning the only three of four major championships he competed in during 1953, has there been a professional golfer who has worked as diligently as Eldrick "Tiger" Woods to develop the best possible golf swing. Hogan labored daily on the driving range, hitting hundreds of practice shots and constantly testing out new setup and swing positions until he developed an antihook swing.

Whereas Hogan depended most on his own instinct to guide him in the search for swing secrets that would allow him to make more solid contact with the ball and hit more fairways off the tee, Woods has always relied on intellect as the guiding force. Throughout his entire golf career, Tiger has sensibly chosen instructors who, based on his own research, would lift his game to the next level. This intelligent approach to learning is what has allowed him to stay confident and strong under the fire of criticism from the golf press, during transitional periods.

The heaviest attacks started after he shocked the golf world by winning the 1997 Masters by twelve shots, then, not long after, announcing that he wanted to change his swing to develop a true *A-game*. Tiger was called everything from cocky to crazy, particularly after going winless in major championships until capturing the 1999 PGA championship. But if that win was not enough to silence the skeptics and prove to them that they were wrong and Tiger was right to change his swing, capturing the Tiger Slam (2000 U.S. Open, 2000 British Open, 2000 PGA and the 2001 Masters) did the trick.

Tiger also won the 2002 Masters and 2002 U.S. Open, which further helped his case, until announcing—to the dismay of avid golfers around the world—that he was once again going to be working on developing an even better swing. Instantly, sports journalists were back pounding the keys of their laptops, again writing lead stories questioning Tiger's motives, and not just to sell copies of the newspaper or magazine they represented. Logically, what Tiger was doing did not make sense, at least to anyone but Tiger.

When Tiger failed to win any of the final two major championships of 2002, then none in 2003 and 2004, sportswriters understandably had a field day. Any other golfer but Tiger, who was so severely scrutinized and questioned again and again about the logic of tinkering with an

Tiger's ability to focus on the target and block out the distractions of the golf gallery when preparing to hit a shot had a lot to do with the boot-camp-type training he received at a young age from his father, Earl Woods.

already winning swing, would certainly have lost their cool, crumbled mentally, or tossed their clubs into a closet and never ever opened its door again. This may sound far-fetched, yet great players, such as two-time U.S. Open champion Curtis Strange and past golfing great Severiano

Ballesteros, gambled with new teachers and swing theories and lost.

The reason Tiger did not fold or cave during press conferences had a lot to do with his father Earl Woods—"Pops"—who trained Tiger from an early age how to be more resilient by purposely trying to distract him during play. Earl's boot-camp type of training included tossing a ball in front of the one Tiger was aiming at, or coughing in the middle of Tiger's swing, or dropping a bag of clubs down on the ground as Tiger was entering the impact zone. Harsh as these tactics seem, they served the purpose of helping Tiger learn how to tune out outside distractions and concentrate on the shot at hand. Consequently, because of Tiger's mental toughness, more often than not the criticism seems to have gone in one ear and out the other.

Tiger's father also taught him to trust his teachers, most notably Rudy Duran, who taught him from ages four to nine, John Anselmo, who coached Tiger from ten until eighteen, and Butch Harmon who worked with Tiger from 1993 to the summer of 2002. Tiger, thus, always had faith in what he was doing under a teacher's guidance, even if his game failed to improve right away.

All of the aforementioned top instructors helped Tiger improve and become a more complete player, so he had no reason to believe that the tips given to him by Hank Haney, the new teacher he first hooked up with in the spring of 2004, would not propel his swing to new and improved heights. Tiger's certainty, based largely on pure ex-

Earl Woods was also a big believer in his son learning and grooving the fundamental movements of the swing, so this new at-the-top position of Tiger's would surely make him proud.

perience, along with a positive attitude, helped him stay focused and remain cool in the line of fire during post-round press conferences.

To understand Tiger's learning process and evolution as a super swinger of a golf club, it's important to appreciate the major technical contributions made by Tiger's father and the trio of extremely qualified PGA instructors that coached him prior to Haney: Duran, Anselmo, and Harmon, in that order.

The biggest contribution made by Earl Woods was teaching Tiger that the setup, or starting position, in golf is governed by the elements of grip, stance, clubface aim, and body alignment. Furthermore, that what's commonly called the address position should be taken very seriously, because to a large degree the setup dictates the type of swing the golfer employs. Tiger's father also taught his son the most fundamental movements of the swing, showing him how to take the club back smoothly, arrive at the top with the club's shaft parallel to the flight line, and trigger the downswing with the lower body. These three keys put Tiger on the right track and gave him the best possible chance of returning the club squarely and solidly to the ball at impact.

Rudy Duran, Tiger's second instructor and head professional at the Heartwell Golf Course in Southern California, changed his grip from a full finger hold to an interlock type hold, the same grip Tiger uses today and, incidentally, the grip that Jack Nicklaus depended on when he was winning major championships. The grip is an element of the setup that Tiger, as well as top pros and top teachers, consider the "engine room" of the swing. You should, too, whether you interlock your right pinky and left forefinger like Tiger does when gripping, or let your right pinky ride atop your left forefinger, like the majority of players do on the PGA, LPGA, Champions, and Nationwide tours.

One chief contribution John Anselmo made as a teacher involved teaching Tiger the art of employing a

Tiger's first professional teacher, Rudy Duran, influenced Tiger to play with an interlock grip, employed by intertwining or interlocking the right pinky and left forefinger, as shown here.

rhythmic to and fro action, by having him hold a range ball basket with both hands and swing it back and through. Anselmo put a basket in Tiger's hands before he had him swing a golf club, knowing that this strategy would teach Tiger to concentrate more on the feel of the swing motion and less on hitting at the ball. Anselmo

TIGER'S NEW SWING

conveyed one magical thought that allowed Tiger to appreciate the value of swinging a basket: "The golf ball will always get in the way of a good swing, and swinging the basket will allow you to develop a great golf technique and hit the ball far and straight." This basket drill will train you to develop an evenly flowing swing motion, controlled by the large muscles of the body, so when practicing this advice follow these same instructions Anselmo gave to Tiger.

Start from a shoulder-width address position, with your weight balanced on the ball of each foot. But, rather than holding a club hold a small, empty, metal driving range basket. Grasp the left side of the basket with the fingers of your left hand, the right side of the basket with the fingers of your right hand. Next, swing back normally, sort of pushing the basket back away from a target you chose at address, while stretching the muscles of your back and left arm. Next, allow your right wrist to hinge rather early in the swing to promote the desired upright action. Finally, swing the basket toward the target you picked out, letting go with the right hand through impact, so you experience an all-important free release action.

Tiger Woods was fortunate to study under Anselmo in his early years, because the man's expertise stretched beyond the scope of knowing how to teach the golf swing. The department of the game that Anselmo excels in is shot-making, and he certainly had a big impact on Tiger, as evidenced by what Tiger said during an interview he did on The Golf Channel: "It's unbelievable how John Anselmo

Tiger's second professional teacher, John Anselmo, played a major role in teaching Tiger to hit creative shots, particularly with irons.

kept things fun and interesting while changing my swing from flat to upright, and teaching me a new shot practically every time he gave me a lesson on the tee or on the course."

What was so different about Anselmo's approach, and why his lessons played such a key role in what Tiger calls "The Process," is that Anselmo encouraged Tiger to depend on mental imagery to help him more easily execute the shot. This is something Tiger's present coach Hank Haney also believes in, having said this in his book, *The Only Golf Lesson You'll Ever Need:*

"You'll play much better with one clear swing thought or an overall feeling or picture of what your swing should feel like and look like."

Most golf insiders credit Butch Harmon, Tiger's third professional coach before Hank Haney took command,

The second Tiger takes the head-cover off his driver, he stares down the fairway, strategizing, as his third professional coach, Butch Harmon (who learned so much about course management from golf legend Ben Hogan), encouraged him to do.

with revamping Tiger's swing and, indeed, Harmon did help Tiger employ a compact, more controlled action that, when timed right, allowed Tiger to drive the ball down the center of fairways and hit iron shots at the flagstick. However, being the creative chameleon that he is, Tiger showed a desire to improve his big swing further, and that is the story of this book. Harmon is, however, a fine teacher and I would be remiss if I did not mention how he also helped Tiger's learning process in the areas of driving strategy and the short game.

Butch was fortunate to have met and played with Ben Hogan, one of golf's all-time best driving strategists and former two-time winner of the prestigious Masters Tournament, played each April at the demanding Augusta National Golf Club course in Augusta, Georgia. Hogan passed on many strategy tips to Butch, and Butch passed these on to Tiger. But that was not all he passed on to his most successful student.

Butch was the son of 1948 Masters champion Claude Harmon, a master around the green, who taught Butch how to handle tough and tricky pitching and chipping situations.

While Butch taught Tiger, he spent a lot of time with him during practice rounds at Augusta National, talking about driving strategy and short-game technique, again based on what he learned from Hogan and his father. This close-up and personal training definitely played a key role in Tiger winning the 1997, 2001, and 2002 Masters championships, and hitting that miraculous chip-in on hole sixteen during the final round of the 2005 Masters, that will go down in history as the "real" winning shot.

Studying at the golf swing schools of Earl Woods, Rudy Duran, John Anselmo, and Butch Harmon, is analogous to a student attending Harvard, Yale, Princeton, and Oxford. Nevertheless, it is not only this exceptional education that has allowed Tiger to become professional golf's dominant player, with nine major championships and countless worldwide tournaments to his credit. Tiger's success early on and even today has a lot to do with a very unique learning process, one involving the mental side of golf rather than the physical side. However, the details have essentially been kept hush-hush by Tiger's camp, possibly because there exists a fear that the golfing public may consider the type of training involved "outside the box."

What I learned about Tiger's mental secrets I include here, because they will allow you stay calm, cool, and collected under extreme pressure, hit on-target shots, and emerge a winner in tournaments or matches at your local club.

At age ten, Earl Woods first introduced Tiger to Captain Jay Brunza, a navy clinical psychologist. According to sportswriters Tim Rosaforte and Ray Oakes, a California golf professional and close friend of Earl Woods, "the Doctor" was apparently brought into Tiger's inner circle, called "Team Tiger," to enhance Tiger's mental game and essentially hypnotize Tiger, the young prodigy that even back then wanted most to one day become so good he could beat Jack Nicklaus's record of eighteen major championships. Rosaforte says he witnessed the hypnotism, and, according to Oakes, Earl told Oakes how Tiger's shotmaking imagination and prowess had been enhanced after just a couple of sessions with Brunza. At that point, Oakes made an appointment to see Brunza.

The fact that Brunza helped Oakes see only a "white carpet fairway" when getting ready to tee off, then swing and hit that fairway time and time again (instead of what he had often done previously in big competitions—focus on water and trees bordering the short grass, make tense golf swings, and hit off-line shots) is incredible enough. But the record shows that what he helped Tiger accomplish is downright amazing.

Brunza was Tiger's on-course psychological guide and caddy during many junior and amateur events that he won, most notably the 1991, 1992, and 1993 U.S. Junior Amateur and the 1994 and 1995 U.S. Amateur. In all, Brunza "looped" for Tiger during thirty-nine matches. "Together," they won thirty-three.

Because I was more shocked to hear reports about Tiger's mental enhancement under Brunza than learning that Muhammad Ali had been hypnotized when he was winning heavyweight championship bouts, I was curious to talk to Brunza.

I actually spoke to Brunza twice. He was brief and concise. "Tiger is now understanding and applying all the high-level mental game keys that I provided him with for many years, and he's mature enough, too, to comprehend the finer points of putting himself into a zone of intense concentration during a round of golf," said Brunza. His well-chosen words confirmed the stories I had been told. Furthermore, our conversations allowed me to understand another reason why Tiger is better than his peers in being able to stay positive while working on a new swing.

After speaking to Brunza, Donna White, a Florida-based hypnotist who has experienced success helping golfers stay positive as they work through the learning process, explained the essence of how hypnosis works.

The hypnotist tells the subject to close their eyes and focus on the body while breathing slowly. Next, using a trigger, such as "You are getting sleepy," the hypnotist leads the subject into a trance that lets the subject "let go" mentally and physically—to sink into the subconscious and erase all negative thoughts and emotions that had previously hindered their concentration and, if they are golfers, their performance on the course.

Hypnosis is a science you can teach yourself, and it's obvious to me after talking to Brunza that Tiger has learned the science, one way or the other. This process allows Tiger to get rid of mental baggage and seemingly explains why he can take in so much swing advice and easily separate golfing facts from golfing fiction.

Another reason for Tiger's mental fortitude, the ability to stay patient and positive when behind—and to keep plugging away until reigning victorious in so many professional tournaments—is meditation. According to John Anselmo, another one of the original members of Team Tiger, since the time Tiger was a young boy he was taught by his Thai mother, Kultida ("Tida"), the principles of Zen. In fact, Tiger's mother gave him a gold Budda chain and explained to him that meditation was exercise for the mind, before taking him to a Buddhist temple in California, where he learned the art of "letting go" from Zen masters.

When you discipline yourself to free the mind, as Tiger and all Buddhists know how to do, you swing freely and hit powerfully accurate shots, rather than letting numerous swing thoughts swim around in your head, tense up, and hit off-line shots. However, first, you must have a good setup and swing base to work from.

The intense, faraway look on Tiger's face during the first hole with Chris DiMarco, at the 2005 Masters playoff, was merely evidence of Tiger experiencing a sense of oneness with the universe that comes with meditation. So it was no surprise, at least to those who really know Tiger, to watch him employ a perfect, new, technically sound, Haney-designed swing on hole eighteen, hit the ball onto the ideal spot of grass on the fairway, play a second shot straight over the flagstick, then hole the winning putt. Everything clicked, due to a stress-free and confident mind-set that Tiger had started grooming years earlier. Tiger had regained his mental edge, but to further appreciate how "The Process" ebbs and flows, let me provide you

Tiger's meditation and work with Navy clinical psychologist Jay Brunza taught him to zone in, and when he took that mind-set and combined it with lessons from new coach Hank Haney, a free and powerful swing action like this was practically a "given."

with some historical anecdotes going back to 1997, when Tiger started to rule the world of professional golf.

Tiger's 1997 victory at Augusta was phenomenal, but what was even more amazing was how, between winning the 1999 PGA and the 2002 U.S. Open, it seemed that when he entered a tournament every other golfer was playing for second place. The second Tiger's name flashed on the leader board, the rest of the players in the field seemed to lose their game and just succumb, much the way an animal grabbed by the jaws of a tiger in the wild knows it faces death and, after an initial struggle, fights no more. Tiger's powerfully accurate tee shots, on-target irons, and pinpoint putts were just so incredible that there really was no golfer in his league. It got to the point where even golf's veteran newspaper and magazine writers put Tiger on such a pedestal that it was suddenly as if legends Bobby Jones, Ben Hogan, and Jack Nicklaus never existed. In short, we all believed that Tiger was superhuman—until the bubble burst and he failed to win any of the remaining majors in 2002, none in 2003, and none in 2004.

Once Tiger blanked out in the U.S. Open, British Open, and PGA championship in 2002, the word "slump" was in practically every sportswriter's column.

By the time 2003 was over, "burnout" was the most popular word in the typical writer's article, and there were cries for Tiger to return to Butch Harmon, or one of his former professional teachers such as John Anselmo, the author of *A-Game Golf*.

Leading into 2004, Tiger put a positive spin on the swing changes he was making with his new coach, Hank Haney, who was the longtime teacher of a two-time major championship winner, and a close friend of Tiger's, Mark O'Meara. Therefore, golf fans who had heard Tiger's optimistic comments during television interviews for The Golf

Channel and during golf telecasts on CBS, ABC, and NBC, were champing at the bit for the 2004 Masters to commence, thinking Tiger would win. Most of the press had turned again in Tiger's favor, believing he was due, as did television golf analysts, top tour pros, and top teachers—except one in particular: Jim McLean.

Because McLean is such a high-profile teacher, runs one of the country's best golf schools, and is a consultant for The Golf Channel, golfers listen when he speaks.

In an article that appeared in *Golf World* magazine on April 9, 2004, McLean claimed that Tiger's swing was overly flat compared to what it was formerly, when Tiger was inarguably the world's greatest golfer. This fault, McLean believed, sometimes caused Tiger to get the club stuck behind him on the downswing and prevented him from consistently hitting the dart-like shots that allowed him to "go low" on the golf course and beat his contemporaries so often that he reached the rare, iconic stature of such legends as Rocky Marciano, Muhammad Ali, Babe Ruth, Marilyn Monroe, and Elvis Presley.

In analyzing Tiger's technique with the help of Carl Welty, a veteran Jim McLean Golf School instructor, McLean wrote that Tiger's swing resembled Mark O'Meara's, and kind of hinted that what Haney taught O'Meara and worked for him did not work for Tiger. Taking things a step further, he made it clear that Tiger should have stuck to the fade shot and not tried to copy O'Meara's draw shot.

"In my opinion, it's difficult for a power player to draw or hook the driver," said Jim McLean in the aforementioned *Golf World* magazine article, which was entitled "Why Is Tiger Woods Struggling?"

"Playing a draw increases the possibility of the two-way (left-or-right) miss. By swinging too much from the inside, you must add more hand action to square the club. In return, when the hands don't release, you put the block (right ball) into play or the big hook (left ball) with too much release, which only requires a minor mistake at Tiger's swing speed."

What was so profound about this article was how McLean backed up his claims by showing how Tiger dropped the club well below the imaginary plane line on the downswing. Furthermore, in a "Tiger By the Numbers" sidebar, McLean showed how Tiger had dropped dramatically in the PGA Tour's distance, accuracy, total driving, greens in regulation, and ball-striking statistics lists.

What is profound, too, is that Tiger himself was seemingly well aware of his drop in the stats and loss record in the major championships, as gathered by what he told the press during the Bay Hill Classic in Orlando, Florida, not long before the 2004 Masters.

"Ninety percent of my shots are really good, it's just that the other ten percent are off the charts."

Tiger's comments frustrated the press, with most reporters shaking their heads and looking bewildered as if wanting to ask Tiger this question: "Why then, do you keep doing what you are doing instead of going back to Butch Harmon and returning to your old swing, so that once again you can win major championships and really give us something exciting to write about?"

I believe the reason that the majority of golf reporters kept quiet and did not say or write what was really on their minds is they wanted Tiger to return to form and raise the level of excitement on the tour by hitting great shots again. They also knew that every time Tiger won a major tournament he would come closer to matching or beating Jack Nicklaus's eighteen major championships record. In addition, they wanted to believe that Tiger was right—that in order to improve at golf, you sometimes must expect to go through bad patches or lulls, until the new changes you incorporate into your swing feel so natural that they do not require any conscious thought to repeat under pressure. The fact is, Tiger was in the process of developing such a swing, one that, once triggered, operates purely, according to the laws of physics, and on automatic pilot. It was just that developing this new swing was taking so long for Tiger to perfect that everyone, except Tiger, was losing their patience.

After Tiger crapped out again in all four major championships in 2004, many golf writers and television golf analysts, such as Jim Nance, never really believed, deep down in their hearts or intellectually, that Tiger would ever return to his old magical form. Nance admitted this during

During "The Process," the club sometimes got "stuck" behind Tiger's body on the downswing (above, left), and this fault often caused him to swing out at the ball (above, right) and hit a block. The fact is, Tiger got his swing back on track, proven by his masterful driving performances and wins at both the 2005 Masters and British Open championships.

the 2005 Masters when, before his eyes, he witnessed Tiger positioning himself to blow out the field. To paraphrase what Nance said, it went something like this:

"I never thought I'd see Tiger return to his great form of 1997, but here he is again, in full control of his game."

Golfers and golf fans who were glued to the television during April 2005, watching the Masters on CBS, now know that Tiger won, but not by a big margin. That was only because Chris DiMarco fought to the end, losing on the first playoff hole to Tiger's winning birdie, earned by hitting a superior tee shot, playing a superior approach into the green, and making a superputt.

As great as Tiger played en route to winning his fourth green jacket—especially during the third round when he was really hot—he'd surely be the first to tell you that he made an unforced error coming down the stretch, a wayward tee shot on the seventeenth hole that cost him winning outright in regulation play, rather than in a playoff. Thankfully, a drive pushed right of target now only creeps into Tiger's game rarely, because he obviously is more comfortable with Haney's way of swinging. And although still in the process of learning, Tiger is a better control player today than before, particularly due to the fact that he has gone from favoring the draw off the tee to favoring the fade. In fact, Tiger's Turbo-Drive fade played a huge role in his 2005 Masters and British Open wins.

Tiger is a very intelligent student of the game, and he carefully selects a teacher and sticks with him as long as he sees improvement. If Tiger had believed that Haney was doing him more harm than good (as some teachers told me prior to Tiger's 2005 Masters victory), he would have broken ties with his new coach. Tiger understands that the process of learning new swing keys and applying them successfully is something that takes time. To support this argument, all you have to do is realize that Tiger's game did not improve overnight when Butch Harmon took over, just as Nick Faldo's swing did not improve right away, once top teacher David Leadbetter was recruited to totally revamp it way back when. Tiger is smart enough to know that, when in search of perfection it is inevitable to experience periods of struggle. He is also experienced enough to know that the wait is worth it, when you come out the other side with a better swing than you had before, and rise to the top, just as Faldo—winning a total of six major championships—had done before him.

Tiger is back on top, yet he will never be satisfied until he breaks Nicklaus's major championship record, so he has more work to do with Haney, a teacher who is only recently come into the limelight, but has been recognized as one of the game's outstanding golf instructors for over a decade. In fact, in 1991, when I was senior editor of instruction at *Golf Magazine*, I put Haney on our publication's prestigious list of the Top 50 Best Teachers in America, after interviewing him and reading his answers to questions we asked all our nominees. Furthermore, in 1996, while still working at *Golf Magazine*, I again voted Haney onto our first America's 100 Best Golf Teachers list.

To understand Tiger's new swing, it's important that you know something about Haney's golf philosophy that has stayed consistent since I first spoke to him. Haney, who now teaches at the Hank Haney Golf Ranch in McKinney, Texas, heavily emphasizes a philosophy that revolves around teaching students to employ an on-plane swing. This makes perfect sense, considering that Ben Hogan's *Five Lessons: The Modern Fundamentals of Golf,* one of

Haney's favorite books, centers around an instructional theme involving swing plane mechanics.

Hogan claimed that the simplest way to understand the plane or angle of the swing was to imagine that, at address, your head is poking through a hole in a large, inclined pane of glass that rests on your shoulders at its top, and on the ground just beyond the ball at the bottom end. Basically, you swing the club back and up on this plane or slightly below it, but never above it. This mental visualization was one of Hogan's well-known keys for swinging on the proper plane and consistently hitting such good golf shots that he earned the reputation as the most powerfully accurate hitter of the 1950s. Hogan's career was highlighted by winning nine major championships, including the 1953 Masters, 1953 U.S. Open, and 1953 British Open, then later revealing his secrets, first in a 1955 *Life* magazine article and, second, in his classic instructional book, *Five Lessons*, published in 1957.

The plane's angle is determined by two factors: the geometry of the club you set behind the ball, and the individual physical characteristics that govern your posture at address. In general, the shorter and the more upright the club, the steeper its angle of inclination as you address the ball, and, therefore, the more upright the swing plane. Conversely, the longer and flatter the lie of the club, the shallower the angle of its inclination at address, and thus the less upright the swing plane. Usually, too, the shorter and stockier the player, the farther away from the ball he or she should stand and the shallower the swing plane will then naturally be. Conversely, if the golfer is tall and slender, he or she will tend to stand closer to the ball and to naturally swing the club on a more upright plane.

If you study the career of Haney it's easy to conclude that one of the reasons for his success is he constantly searches for new knowledge. He found what he was looking for from two teachers he claims had the biggest influence on his teaching: John Jacobs and Jim Hardy. Furthermore, like these two mentors, Haney has his own take on swing planes, saying this in his book, *The Only Golf Lesson You'll Ever Need:* "There is more than one plane in the perfect golf swing, but only one plane angle."

John Jacobs, a teacher from England who I had the pleasure of meeting when I worked in London, first as a freelance writer for *Par Golf* magazine, then as an editor for *Golf Illustrated* magazine, took swing philosophy to a new level when he wrote a groundbreaking book, *Practical Golf,* in 1972. Instead of focusing on the club swinging on plane, he advised golfers to focus on swinging the arms up on an upright plane while rotating the shoulders more around, on a flat plane.

Jacobs, the father of the two-plane swing, had a big influence on American Jim Hardy. And not long after Jacobs's book was published, Hardy became Haney's first serious teacher. At that time, Haney was a freshman in college and member at Exmoor Country Club in Highland Park, Illinois, where Hardy was the head golf professional.

Hardy ended up running several golf schools and eventually became the director of the John Jacobs Golf Schools. Hardy hired Haney to be one of his teachers, especially since his protégé had become an expert at teaching the two-plane swing. Ironically, though, Hardy liked to experiment even more than Haney, and he started working on a one-plane swing theory. Basically, in a one-plane swing, the arms swing around the body on the backswing, essentially on the same plane as the shoulders.

Hardy and Haney worked together for years, until, around 1986, Haney went to the PGA West golf resort in Palm Springs, California, to teach, taking with him the knowledge he learned from Jacobs and Hardy.

Haney started entering the limelight in 1998, when his star student Mark O'Meara, who for so long had been called the best player never to win a major championship, captured two in one year, the Masters and the British Open.

Hardy first returned to the limelight in 2003, when his longtime student Peter Jacobsen won the Hartford Open at age forty-nine, then a year later, when "Jake" won the U.S. Senior Open—thanks to switching to a one-plane action that Hardy had figured out, mastered, then passed on to Jacobsen.

"The one-plane swing is best envisioned as a baseball swing at the ground," according to Hardy, author of the best-selling book, *The Plane Truth for Golfers*.

"The spine is bent over, the shoulders are turning on

Pow! Solid shots like this (above) sure have silenced the critics, proving the new Woods-Haney team (opposite page) works well together.

an inclined plane, and the arms are swinging across the chest."

Although Hardy and Haney go way back, it was Hardy who first criticized Tiger's swing in 2003, although constructively, because he knew only too well that it was truly a work in progress. Hardy's major criticism was that Tiger's arm-swing had gotten too far from his body on the backswing. This type of backswing action, as Hardy

pointed out, occasionally causes Tiger problems on the downswing, especially when swinging a driver.

"The most common bad thing occurs when Tiger doesn't drop his arms enough to the inside," wrote Hardy in a November 2003 *Golf Digest* article.

"With his body sensing that the downswing path is headed out to in, Tiger compensates by keeping the club's face open and wiping across the ball, producing the block fade that he has hit so often lately.

"When Tiger returns to the ball by dropping his arms too far inside the proper plane, it results in the so-called 'stuck position' he bemoans. Now the club is entering the hitting area from inside to out, forcing Tiger to rotate his hands in an attempt to save the shot from going right. What often ensues is a shot that goes left."

In 2004, when observing Tiger, Hardy wondered

whether he would become a pure one- or two-plane swinger, spotting elements of both type of swings in his action.

In June of 2005, after observing him at Pinehurst, Hardy told me that Tiger employed a one-plane body turn with a two-plane arm swing, and that the only reliable shot you can hit with this action when using a driver is a fade. That just so happens to be the bread-and-butter shot that has turned Tiger's tee-ball game around and allowed him to regain his number-one spot in the world of professional golf.

There has been no official comment from Haney as to whether or not he considered what Hardy teaches when instructing Tiger. Yet, one thing is certain: Tiger now has the best on-plane swing in golf, and because it is so unique, and because Tiger is also so savvy and strong-willed, there's no doubt in my mind that he had something to say about adding his own little nuances into the mix when configuring this new technique.

Let's look at Tiger's special swing by first analyzing his new setup, then moving on to his highly innovative backswing and downswing actions, then we will review the drills that have enabled Tiger, and will enable you, to develop a new, more efficient golf swing.

2. SETTING UP FOR POWER
AND CONTROL

Use Tiger's unique setup position to promote controlled,
hard-hit shots.

n 1997, when I wrote the book *The Tiger Woods Way,*
which analyzed Tiger's power-swing technique, he was
looked upon as a golfing wizard, especially after he won
the Masters in April of that same year—by twelve shots!

Because of my background as a former golf instructor
and senior editor of instruction at *Golf Magazine,* I was especially curious to dig deep and figure out the special features of Tiger's golf swing that set it apart from swings
used by other golf professionals who compete week after
week on the PGA Tour. So, more in the manner of Her-
cule Poirot, Agatha Christie's inquisitive fictional French
detective, than a golf analyst, I questioned Tiger's fellow
tour players, top teachers from the PGA of America and
the United States Golf Teachers Federation, television

swing analysts, and low-handicap amateur players. In addition, I viewed videotapes and stacks of photographs, showing Tiger swinging, and watched him practice and play at tournaments. In search of Tiger's setup and swing secrets, I even looked through a special magnifying glass called a "loop," used by artists and jewelers, to examine frame-by-frame photographic sequence shots showing his technique. I had to, since I wanted desperately to answer this question: How does Tiger hit the ball so powerfully and accurately with right-to-left draw flight?

In my heart, I felt that Tiger had more than one swing secret to hitting super-controlled power-draw drives off the tee. But in my head, I thought it was just one, perhaps nondetectable secret that I would never discover.

Realizing that the setup or address position plays a major role in the type of swing a golfer ultimately employs, I began my investigation by closely examining Tiger's starting position.

After conducting a tremendous amount of research and making pages of notes, I solved the mystery, and although Tiger now has a brand new and better action, I feel that it is vital for me to share his old secrets with you. That way, you will establish an important reference point for understanding how Tiger's former setup and swing worked and why, eventually, he chose to change it.

Tiger's chief secret involved setting up to the ball with his feet aiming slightly right of target (in a closed position), and his shoulders pointing left of target (in an open position). Setting up with his feet closed allowed Tiger to turn his hips freely in a clockwise direction and swing the club back on an inside path. The open shoulder position enabled Tiger to clear his entire left side more fully and briskly on the downswing.

When I completed my research, I determined that only one other great player in the history of the game, Sam Snead, set up like Tiger. However, Snead was not as long off the tee and did not hit iron shots as powerfully as Tiger. The reason is Tiger generated faster club-head speed and hit the ball with a more severe draw flight. More importantly, he imparted a larger degree of "hot" overspin on the ball, so, once landing, it bounded hard on the fairway and rolled farther than the soft-draw shots hit by former legend Sam Snead.

The other technical factors that allowed Tiger to hit a superpowerful draw included a strong grip, light grip pressure, a flatter swing plane than Snead's, together with an exaggerated clockwise rotation of the right forearm, right wrist, and right hand through impact. This unique release action causes the toe of the club to lead its heel in the hit zone and impart exaggerated draw spin on the ball.

In conducting further research for the book, I went back and analyzed both Tiger and Snead's actions more closely, determining that, although Snead did not hit the ball as far as Tiger, he was more in control of the golf ball's flight than Tiger and hit a higher percentage of fairways off the tee. That was due largely to Snead holding the club with a neutral grip and more firmly, swinging back on a more upright plane, taking longer to clear his hips on the downswing, and employing a slower release of the club in the hitting area. In fact, while Tiger's club moved in a flash through impact and his hitting action was explosive, Snead's swing was so syrupy it looked effortless.

To say that Snead was smarter than Tiger is unfair, but to say that Snead was a more natural player than Tiger is not unfair. Snead's supersmooth, self-taught swing action was truly poetry in motion. Tiger's old swing was modeled after his father's and grooved through long practice sessions over years and years. Sure, when Tiger's old swing was on, no tour professional hit the ball as far with such control. In fact, he won eight major championships with that swing. The thing is, what golf fans missed is what Tiger was surely fully aware of: when Tiger's swing was off, he usually hit at least one off-line hook per round, but often managed to win anyway, owing to hitting miraculous recovery shots. However, we now know that all the time he must have been keeping records and thinking about one day having to change to a more consistent setup and swing, just as Ben Hogan had done before him, to remove that damaging hook from his game. Sure, when you time this shot just right it goes a mile, but when you are a little bit off the ball bounds into deep trouble. On the PGA Tour, you cannot hit this shot for too long without it finally catching up to you and causing you harm, score-wise, which is exactly what started happening to Tiger. What's so ironic about Tiger's old winning swing is that what was so good about it was what was also so bad about it. Tiger's former action required great strength, extreme flexibility, and superb hand-eye coordination, all the qualities that Tiger possessed. All the same, Tiger's old swing was like an antique grandfather clock with a complex mechanism. To keep good time, every single part of his body had to move in a perfectly synchronized manner. No other swing in golf depended so much on tempo, timing, and rhythm as Tiger's. The main reason this was true was that Butch Harmon believed that a shallow swing action was better than an upright action. The only thing is, with this type of backswing the club travels along a longer path, making it much harder for it to be directed down squarely into the ball.

"The driver must meet the ball with a level plane," wrote Harmon in the book *The Four Cornerstones of Winning Golf*.

"For the club to be moving through impact on a shallow angle, the entire swing must be on a relatively shallow plane, a little more around the body than up and down."

Harmon teaches students to create the desired flatter swing by moving a triangle formed by the arms and shoulders and extending the club back on a wide arc, while not overdoing hip action. Incidentally, Harmon made a point of telling me that his dad told him that the golfer who spins the right hip on the backswing or the left hip on the downswing will never be a consistent winner.

Two elements of Tiger's old swing—taking the club back on an exaggerated inside path early in the backswing (above, left) and clearing his hips too soon on the downswing (above, right). Both could be traced to his closed-foot position at address, and they triggered some serious shot-making problems.

Tiger heeded Harmon's advice and played great golf for a good many years, yet slowly but surely he slipped into bad habits, namely pulling the club well inside the target line early in the backswing (while exaggerating the coiling action of the right hip) and clearing or spinning his hips too quickly on the downswing.

Harmon has a great eye for spotting faults in a golf swing. I know that from playing with him. I've had a lot of good days on the golf course. For example, once while playing golf with British Open and Masters winner Sandy Lyle at his home course, Hawkstone Park in Shropshire, England, I shot a score of 2 under par 70 to his 68, and had not one score over par on any hole—two birdies and sixteen pars. Another time, playing with legendary golfer Severiano Ballesteros, I shot 77 to his 74 on the par-74 La Manga course in Spain. And I shot a course record score of 68 at the Crab Meadow Golf Course on Long Island, New York. But on the day I played with Butch on my former home course of Lake Nona Golf Club in Orlando, Florida, I hit the ball horribly. After the round, Butch pinpointed my faults, provided me with some pointers, and fixed my swing. Take it from me, or some of his students such as pros Adam Scott and Justin Leonard, Harmon's a super teacher.

I doubt very much if Butch would have not noticed Tiger's swing faults. The question is, did he allow Tiger to continue swinging this way, on an exaggerated flat plane, in the hope that Tiger would continue to make correct compensatory movements and the time the downswing so perfectly that he would continue to hit good shots practically all of the time? And, if so, did his strategy backfire, or did he suggest to Tiger that his swing was off, and for whatever reason Tiger kept swinging the same way, also hoping for the best? These are valid questions; however, because both Butch and Tiger have been virtually silent on the subject of the swing, I have been forced to draw my own conclusions, which, as an instructional expert, I thankfully am able to do.

The fact that I don't know really doesn't matter. What does matter is that the more Tiger swung the club back on too flat a path and plane, the more he coiled his hips, and, in turn, the harder it became for him to return the club to a square impact position, no matter how fast he uncoiled his hips on the downswing. The club lagged so far behind his racing lower body, hands, and arms, that Tiger got "stuck." When this happens, and it is a helpless feeling, as you might know, the player fears hitting a block shot right of target and compensates by releasing the right forearm too vigorously. The club's face then closes at impact, instead of squaring up to the ball and target. The result is a severe hook shot. What's so crazy about this problem is this: when Tiger or any other good player feels their hips moving so quickly on the downswing, he or she knows that a hook is inevitable, so their natural reaction is to slow the release to try and prevent the left-to-right shot. The result, ironically, is a severe right-to-right slice shot.

Tiger experienced these problems and finally chose to seek out a new teacher, Hank Haney, and to solve his problems by rebuilding his swing from the ground up. So, when all is said and done, it's apparent that Tiger ended up leaving Butch Harmon and turning to Haney in order to develop a swing that prevented him from hitting a score-wrecking hook when his timing was just a little bit off.

Like Ben Hogan before him, Tiger was looking for a

swing that requires less maintenance to master, relies less on timing, and produces a shot that travels left-to-right in the air, or fades, and hits the fairway a high percentage of the time.

The first step to developing such a new swing—one that will provide you with more margin of error and allow you to hit more on-target tee shots—is a new and improved setup position.

Changing setup positions was a big gamble for Tiger (and teacher Hank Haney) and required some hard practice, so it's understandable that nearly three years passed between winning his eighth and ninth major championships.

Whenever a golfer incorporates even one simple change into his address position, such as changing his grip from strong (V's formed by the thumbs and forefingers point up at the player's right shoulder) to weak (V's point up at the player's right ear), it takes some getting used to. Tiger changed many elements of his setup, including his preswing routine, and if anyone else does the same they shouldn't expect instant magic.

The one noticeable difference when observing Tiger's routine is that he seems to be taking a lot more time to prepare for a shot. He stands behind the ball and stares down the fairway, apparently imagining a well-hit shot flying straight down the middle of the short grass or working its way slightly from left to right. Next, he employs a couple of miniature swings to loosen up his muscles, get a feel for

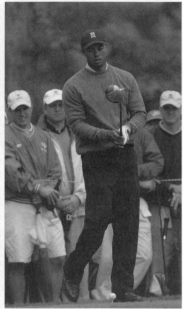

In preparing to drive, Tiger now employs miniature practice swings (above, left) and quietly steps into the shot (above, right).

the club, and establish a smooth rhythm. Then he steps quietly into the setup, just like the great Ben Hogan did, to give himself a little extra time to prepare mentally for the shot.

When Tiger was off his game, I noticed that he was rushing his routine, but on the last day of the 2005 Masters, he was taking his time and not stepping into the shot until, I suspect, he was 100 percent sure he was going to make the good swing and hit the good shot he imagined himself hitting in his mind's eye. At Augusta National Tiger was grinding so hard that more than one CBS color analyst commented about the noticeable difference in Tiger's routine.

One teacher I spoke to, who chose to speak off the record, said Tiger was taking longer because his setup and swing were still new and he had to think harder about what he was doing. Well, there's probably some truth to this, but not all that much. That's because, in order to hit quality golf shots, you can't afford to think out the swing. You can only do that in practice, when you are learning new swing movements. On the course, you must let go and let the swing happen.

Judging from the high number of great shots Tiger is hitting these days, his mind is clear of any deep, technical thoughts, and his swing action is certainly on cruise control. How do I know that? Well, just listen to this comment Tiger made during a special feature that aired on The Golf Channel in June 2005: "A lot of the time I don't hear noise, because I'm so in the moment preparing for a shot, almost as if I get out of the way," said Tiger.

If you stick to one highly grooved, regimented, preswing routine, one Tiger's former mental coach Jay Brunza calls the "forty-second sanctuary," you will make many more good swings than bad swings. The same preswing routine prepares your subconscious mind for the best possible repetition of the swing you intend to employ. That's because, if the brain recognizes exactly what actions the body intends to make and the exact order in which each and every complex movement will be employed, the swing tends to flow correctly and automatically without any further conscious direction.

"The key is to build yourself a routine that works for you," said Hank Haney in the book, *The Only Golf Lesson You'll Ever Need*. "Then stick with it. Do it every time you hit a shot on the course."

It's obvious that Haney has reinforced what Tiger's father and Tiger's former professional teachers, Rudy Duran, John Anselmo, and Butch Harmon, stressed about the value of a preswing routine; plus he's given Tiger some new tips too, because Tiger sure looks more serious when preparing to hit a shot, particularly his new signature Turbo Drive. It's also apparent that Tiger believes in what Haney says about sticking to the same routine, because if something doesn't feel right or if anything disturbs his preparatory routine, he stops and starts all over again.

That's what you should do. I say that knowing from my own experience and talking to tour pros, that if you even add one more waggle to your routine, "milk" your grip a few more times than normal, or increase the number of practice swings you typically employ, the subconscious mind becomes perplexed. Your lesson: Step away and start your routine over, otherwise your swing will short-circuit and you'll hit a bad shot.

The next time you are sitting on your couch or at your country club watching golf, or watching Tiger playing in person at a tournament, take note of how methodically and quietly he prepares for a shot. Like Jack Nicklaus, the most meticulous player in the history of the game, Tiger adheres to a preswing routine that in its most basic form includes the following steps:

1. Tiger stands a couple of yards behind the ball, staring down the fairway to determine the ideal landing area and "see" the best shape of shot to hit.

2. Tiger makes a couple of miniswings to get a feel for the club, establish good rhythm, and relax the muscles.

3. Tiger steps into the shot very quietly, setting the driver head behind the ball so that its face is perpendicular to an area of fairway where, ideally, the ball will land.

4. Tiger jockeys his feet and body into an open position, then bends over slightly at the waist and flexes his knees slightly. (It's important to note that Tiger now stands taller to the ball, with his feet spread only shoulder-width apart, to help promote a more upright swing action.)

5. Tiger looks down at the club to see if it is lined up square.

6. Tiger looks up at the target.

7. Tiger looks back down at the ball.

8. Tiger looks back up at the target.

9. Tiger looks back down at the ball.

Starting at the target and "seeing the shot" is a very critical step in Tiger's preswing routine.

Tiger has said during press conferences that he just "sees the shot and hits it," and I believe him. But it would not be possible for Tiger to hit quality shots that fly straight or fade slightly in the air—shots that allowed him to make a comeback, highlighted by his 2005 Masters and 2005 British Open wins—if he did not listen to Haney's advice on how to set up to the ball in a brand-new way, a way that promotes a more upright swing and a controlled power-fade shot.

As talented and athletic as Tiger is, when he studied the swing under teacher Butch Harmon and won eight major championships, hitting a bread-and-butter draw shot, his good form did not last. During a slump period, highlighted by nearly a three-year no-win record in major championships, he obviously learned the hard way that the right-to-left shot draw is a much more difficult shot to hit consistently than a left-to-right power fade, which is precisely why such golfing greats as Jack Nicklaus, Ben Hogan, and Lee Trevino depended on the fade throughout their careers.

In commenting on his new turbo drive swing in the May 2005 issue of *Golf Digest*, Tiger talked about how far he is now hitting the ball, the advantages of his new swing, and the type of shot he hits.

"I'm even driving par 4s—like the 330-yard sixteenth hole at Doral this year and the 320-yard sixth hole at Oakland Hills during the Ryder Cup," said Tiger.

"The big difference is that my misses are playable now. My accuracy has improved mostly because my ball flight is either straight or slightly left-to-right. The fade is a go-to shot I can bomb out there and keep in play."

It's amazing how Tiger succeeded in making such a dramatic switch, from a draw to a fade, because it required him to virtually totally revamp his setup and swing. In your case, making the switch is likely to be easier than it was for Tiger. Now I know that shocks you, so let me explain how good can sometimes come out of bad.

Chances are, you are a middle- to high-handicap player, as are the majority of the 27 million American golfers who play this game. It is likely, too, that you already hit the ball from left to right, albeit in a more severe push or slice pattern; yet, provided your timing is generally good during a round of golf, you can pretty much control the flight of the ball, even though, admittedly, it curves right, causing you to lose vital distance. If I speak the truth, don't worry, for it is not as hard as it sounds to change your setup and swing, and to then turn your shots into a strong power fade. Moreover, you do not need the advanced athletic skills that are required for making a switch from a fade to a draw.

The first step to making a change to a power-fade type shot, or a straight shot, depending on the nature of your release (real slow for the fade, stronger but still smooth for the straight shot), is to match your setup to Tiger's. So let's now look at the elements of this golfing virtuoso's address position.

In order to hit a power-fade shot like Tiger, it's essential that you swing the club on a more upright plane, which, again, many of you may already be doing. If so, however, you probably go a little too far by lifting the club up on too steep a plane. Following Tiger's example will put a stop to your bad habits and literally set you on the proper path to improvement.

To program an upright plane into your setup, use a weak grip like Tiger's, with the Vs formed by your thumbs

Here you see how Tiger's weak grip (above, left) helps Tiger tilt the club shaft up at the start of the swing (above, right), a prerequisite for swinging on an upright rather than flat plane.

and forefingers pointing up at your right ear as described earlier. For some reason, should this hold fail to give you the desired results, try a more extreme weak grip, like that used by former golfing great Ben Hogan. As a matter of interest, Hogan's left-hand V pointed up at his right eye while the V of his right hand pointed up at his chin. As I wrote in my book, *The Hogan Way,* golfing great Byron Nelson and other experts believed this extreme change prevented Hogan from closing the club's face at the top of the swing and at impact, thereby stopping his hook problem. Teaching guru David Leadbetter, best known for revamping the swing of Nick Faldo, agrees that Hogan's right-hand grip ultimately prevented the toe of the club from passing its heel through impact and promoting a hook shot that Hogan feared most. My suggestion: keep moving your hands toward the target slightly and see what type of weak grip works best.

"The correct grip for you is the one that delivers your clubface square to your direction of swing during impact," said one of Haney's teaching idols John Jacobs, in his classic book, *Practical Golf*.

Jacobs went on to say that the golfer should experiment to see which grip works best, and I agree with this advice.

Whether you copy Tiger's weak grip or feel better using Hogan's is a very personal choice. The important thing is to work on your grip and adopt some version of the weak grip, because it will help you swing on a more upright plane. That's why the grip is called the "engine room" of the swing. It allows you to swing the club back on a plane shaped more like a Ferris wheel than a merry-go-round, to borrow an image from teaching great John Jacobs. This, of course, is opposite to the way Tiger swung when taking lessons from Harmon, but it is the best plane shape, according to Jack Nicklaus.

"An upright plane gives the golfer his best chance of swinging the club along the target line at impact," said Nicklaus in his bestselling book *Golf My Way*.

Tiger's old strong grip encouraged him to swing the club on an exaggerated inside path and flat plane. That often prevented him from squaring the club's face at impact.

His new weak grip allows him to swing the club on a more manageable upright plane and return the club solidly into the back of the ball at impact.

I'll present you with a detailed account of Tiger's upright plane and how it applies to driver play in chapter 3; however, first let me explain how his new way of gripping and swinging also make him a more effective player when hitting shots from a rough bordering the fairway.

Your new swing will make you more accurate off the tee, yes, but even Tiger and other top professionals usually miss some fairways during a round of golf. However, like Tiger, you will turn into a better recovery player by changing your swing plane to a more upright one. This short anecdote will prove my point.

In route to winning his fourth Masters, at Augusta National Golf Club, in April 2005, Tiger hit shots that flew high and landed softly on the putting surface, while other pros playing from rough hit the ball heavy or hit shots that flew off the club's face and carried the green. You'll hit super recovery shots, too, once you switch to an upright action. The reason is that when the club approaches the ball from this more upright angle there's less chance that long grass will wrap around the club's neck and slow its momentum, muffling the shot. Also, with the upright swing, less grass gets lodged between the club and the ball at impact, so you are able to impart new backspin to the ball.

Two other creative features of Tiger's setup that promote the ideal upright swing plane are pointing his right

Before taking lessons from Hank Haney, Tiger set up with his hands behind the ball (top), which caused him to extend the club back too far and tense up his arms (bottom).

foot virtually perpendicular to the target line and setting up with the back of his left hand slightly ahead of the ball. When setting up to drive, Tiger used to fan his right foot out quite a lot and set his hands well behind the ball. His new setup features help him greatly, evidenced by his renewed fine play.

Where Tiger's right foot points may seem like a minor

detail, but it encourages the desired upright plane, plus it acts as a sort of backstop that prevents his hips from over-turning on the backswing and spinning out on the down-swing.

Tiger's new hand position encourages him to set the wrists earlier and swing the club back on the desired nar-rower arc, whereas, prior to going to Haney for lessons Tiger had too much extension or "width" to his back-swing. This new hand position promotes relaxation in the arms, and that's a good thing because, as top teacher Jim McLean says, "Spaghetti arms promote an uninhibited ac-celerated swing action." And there's no doubt Tiger's club accelerates at extreme speed in the impact zone—around 130 miles per hour.

Before getting into what I truly believe is Tiger's ulti-mate secret, I'd like to review some other aspects of Tiger's new setup that play a key role in promoting an on-plane, on-path, powerfully accurate swinging motion.

Tiger is very athletic and balanced at address, because he's bending less at the knees and from the ball and socket joints of his hips. This new posture seems to be giving Tiger a sense of freedom when swinging the club up and down along an upright plane, and it further prevents him from becoming tense and feeling trapped in the hitting area of the downswing. To get a visual sense of Tiger's pos-ture, look at him standing at address. You can see he is in what legendary golfer Severiano Ballesteros calls a position "halfway between a soldier's attention and at-ease posi-

Tiger's new right-foot position and athletic posture allow him to swing the club back freely on an upright plane, with his right wrist now hinging sooner and less tension is his arms.

tions." Furthermore, there's now less of an angle created between his upper and lower body—about twenty degrees instead of thirty. Tiger's posture at address may seem inconsequential, but it is most important that it be precise in order for him to swing the club in a consistent manner, with symmetry on the backswing and downswing.

Hank Haney, Tiger's coach, stresses symmetry in the swing, calling for the club to swing along the plane angle early in the backswing, parallel to the plane angle later in the backswing, parallel to the plane angle early in the downswing, then along the plane angle in the impact zone. No other teacher, except perhaps one of Haney's mentors, Jim Hardy, ever understood the concept of plane as clearly as Haney and explained it so concisely.

Something else that I found interesting when studying Tiger's address is that, in contrast to other professionals on the PGA Tour, he sets his left shoulder much higher than his right. Teachers talk all the time about level shoulders. However, Tiger's new, more pronounced high-shoulder position is a technical nuance that causes his upper body weight to lean right. So Tiger's body is preset to deliver the club to the ball on the upswing, and because Tiger now plays the ball more forward in his stance than previously, the strike is clean and supersolid. This type of hitting action is much different than what is taught by the majority of top teachers today, so it's obvious Haney and Woods know something they don't know. The typical teaching professional wants the club to move low to the ground just before and just after impact. The phrase used to describe such movement is "flat spot," and teachers claim that the player who employs this low-moving club action is able to keep the club's face on the ball a split second longer and hit the ball farther. I once agreed with this philosophy, too; but Tiger is living proof that it holds no water. Besides, in order to create a flat spot in the hit zone you have to extend the club back low in the takeaway for approximately eighteen inches. I used to also think this extended takeaway was the way to go, but I no longer think that a wide arc is the best way to build power in the swing. I believe, after ana-lyzing Tiger's new swing, that it is best to set the wrists early in the backswing and hit the ball on the upswing. I believe, too, that you will soon see a lot of Tiger's fellow professionals copying him and golf instructors also starting to adopt the early-set and turn philosophy.

The early set of the wrist feels more natural and keeps the hands, wrists, and arms so relaxed and alive that when it comes time to hit the ball on the upswing a maximum degree of club-head speed and power is generated.

You'll understand this concept more clearly when read-ing chapter 4 on the downswing. For now, however, let me just say that when you hit the ball in a Tiger-like fashion you are able to hold your wrist-hinge position and weight back, until the last final moment when the wrists straighten and you throw all your weight into the shot. Once you un-derstand these swing keys more fully and how to apply them, I bet you will compare the through-impact action to throwing a powerful and mean uppercut punch.

Although I have certainly cited some new elements of Tiger's setup, I believe that the real secret to how he hits powerful shots off the tee, certainly what he refers to as the Turbo Drive, involves a unique body alignment position. So unique, in fact, that I just can't believe top teacher and television golf analyst Peter Kostis neglected to cite this feature of Tiger's new setup when comparing Tiger's old and new swings in a July 2005 *Golf Magazine* article enti-tled "Tigerize Your Swing."

Now, when hitting a fade, rather than a draw, Tiger sets his feet in an open position (rather than closed as he did before when setting up), and keeps his shoulders slightly open to the target line but dead square to the line the ball will start flying on. This address position is different than that used by three of the most legendary drivers of the ball, Ben Hogan, Sam Snead, and Jack Nicklaus. Hogan set his feet closed and his shoulders square to the target. Snead set his feet closed and his shoulders open. Nicklaus set both his feet and shoulders quite dramatically open, though his setup comes closet to Tiger's.

I've observed this secret myself, from studying Tiger's setup. I did not gather this information from any top

Tiger's new setup (below, left) allows him to swing on an upright plane (below, right) and hit a Turbo-Drive fade shot.

teacher, tour player, or television swing analyst. But as you can see, when looking at the photograph showing Tiger's address, it's true. Furthermore, once you try it, you'll see it works wonders in automatically promoting a good swing. So it will not surprise me if teachers soon stop telling students to set their feet and body square or parallel to the target line.

Setting up Tiger-style promotes the desired upright plane. Moreover, it prevents you from overturning the hips and in turn losing torque, or swinging the club on such a flat path that it is impossible to return the club square to the target without making compensatory moves that are difficult for even Tiger to make consistently.

Setting up with your feet and shoulders open will allow you to start the club back slightly outside the target line, just like Tiger. However, once your shoulders start turning clockwise they will turn into a square position, and keep the club moving back on the correct upright plane and square path, rather than back and around the body. This new setup will put you in position, early on, to return the club to the ball squarely at impact, and prevent you from making a critical error in the takeaway. Those of you who set your feet and body squarely, then, once turning your shoulders clockwise, get the club stuck behind you in a position that you can't recover from, will no longer experience this problem. Those of you who set your feet and shoulders well open to the target line, as opposed to just slightly, like Tiger, will no longer tend to lift the club up on too steep a plane, swing across the ball at impact, and hit a vicious slice shot.

Imagine, after all these years, Tiger is just now learning to swing on a pure plane, which explains why he's hitting a higher percentage of good shots. Setting up Tiger's way will allow the plane of your swinging left arm, the golf club, and your left shoulder to match up, and if it's swing symmetry that teacher Hank Haney wants out of Tiger and other students, this is one, sure shortcut to achieving that goal—practically foolproof, in fact.

3. GETTING YOUR BACKSWING BACK ON TRACK

To swing back on a unique circular upright plane like Tiger, so you are poised to employ a powerful, on-balanced downswing action, learn and groove this golfing super-star's new body-club positions.

E arly on in their teacher-student relationship, Butch Harmon suggested Tiger make some big changes to his backswing action. Tiger was willing to listen to Harmon because he thought he needed to develop a better swing after losing the 1993 U.S. Amateur Championship in Houston, Texas. Besides, he had heard from his father and others that Butch had done great things for Greg Norman, one of Tiger's favorite players. This was not surprising, when you consider that Butch came from good stock. His father, the late Claude Harmon Sr., is considered one of the all-time best golf instructors, which explains why he taught at two of America's finest golf clubs: Seminole in

Palm Beach, Florida and Winged Foot in Mamaroneck, New York.

It's ironic that two or three of the changes Butch made to Tiger's swing went against what Tiger had been taught by John Anselmo, the low-keyed teacher from Huntington Beach, California, who groomed Tiger's game from the age of ten until eighteen. During the years Anselmo taught Tiger, his star student won the 1988, 1989, 1990, and 1991 World Junior Championship, the 1991, 1992, and 1993 U.S. Junior Amateur, and the 1994 U.S. Amateur.

Anselmo had trained Tiger to set the wrists early in the backswing, swing the club to the parallel position by using the muscles of his back to control the action, and to keep the left wrist flat at the top. As Anselmo advised Tiger long ago, when you stretch the back muscles you are virtually guaranteed of making a full backswing and balancing your weight correctly on your right foot and leg. (Conversely, when you use the hands to control the backswing and concentrate on employing a three-quarter action, the tendency is to lift the club up on too steep an angle and leave your weight on your left side during the backswing, then on your right side on the downswing. This is opposite to what should be done. When Tiger started going bad, it was this faulty backswing that caused him to come into impact with the club's face open, and to hit high, weak shots— weak by Tiger's standards, anyway. Alternatively, fearing a weak push or even slice, Tiger would sometimes flip his

Even Tiger learned that trying to employ a three-quarter swing can lead to tee-shot problems.

right hand and right wrist over counterclockwise, shut the club's face, and hit an uncontrollable hook.)

Anselmo explained to Tiger (as he does his new, junior star student, Jim Liu) that the early set of the wrists enables the swing to stay smooth and upright, and also enables the arms to stay flexible enough to act as power sources.

Harmon, on the other hand, suggested Tiger extend the arms and club back early in the backswing and swing to the three-quarter position, with his left wrist cupped (marked by an indentation or "cup" between the back of the left forearm and left hand). Harmon believed what Hogan believed: if the left wrist is cupped at the top, the club's face will open up on the backswing. So, no matter how hard you swing down, you will not be able to hook the ball. Well, for years this worked, but as I have hinted before, eventually this swing strategy backfired. Anselmo told me that he expected this would happen and even told Earl Woods that Tiger's cupped left wrist position would lead to directional problems off the tee.

When Tiger first came to Anselmo for lessons in the spring of 1986, he was quite short in stature and had been swinging a cut-down two-and-one-half wood that was still long enough to promote an overly rounded swing. Later on, when Tiger turned thirteen, he started sprouting upward fast, so Tiger wanted to swing on a more upright plane. The trouble was he had trouble doing this. Consequently, Anslemo had to replane Tiger's swing and helped him get rid of the bad habit of cupping his left wrist at the top, which caused the club's face to open rather than remain square.

"I made Tiger's swing more upright by having him stand closer to the ball, and by telling him to raise his hands a little higher and bring them closer in to his body at address," said Anselmo in *A-Game Golf,* a book that's soon to be available on DVD.

"I also instructed Tiger to set his hands above his right

This new, full, upright swing of Tiger's, learned under his coach, Hank Haney, would surely please Tiger's former instructor John Anselmo, who stresses that students swing their hands higher than the level of the right shoulder at the top.

shoulder at the completion of the backswing, rather than behind his back. After about a week, Tiger got used to swinging on a more upright plane, which is the angle of the swing I prefer."

If you have been reading very closely and following my instructions, you can see already that some of the swing keys that Anselmo taught Tiger are the very same ones that Hank Haney teaches him now. This seems ironic, but there's more to the story.

In late 2004, when Tiger was struggling with his game, John Anselmo was visiting his dear friend Earl Woods at his home. The phone rang. Tiger was on the line. Earl passed the phone to Anselmo and, according to Anselmo, this time they talked golf-swing technique.

Now, Tiger had seen John quite often since he had become a major championship winner. John even flew to Scotland to follow Tiger and talk to him during the 2000 British Open that Tiger won at St. Andrews. He was also asked to join Tiger and teach at a Tiger Woods Foundation clinic in 2001. But on each of those occasions the two of them did not seriously discuss Tiger's golf game. However, during the aforementioned telephone conversation, Anselmo told Tiger that he was not balancing his weight fully and correctly on his right leg at the top of the backswing and not planting his left foot firmly enough at the start of the downswing, which, in turn, was causing him to spin out, lose his balance, and hit off-line shots. Since Tiger has now improved these aspects of his swing, it goes without saying that Anselmo was partially responsible for rekindling the fire in Tiger's golf game and bringing him back to his old form.

One more thing, though: Anselmo also told Tiger that he should return to using a steel-shafted driver, since he believed the graphite-shafted one Tiger was swinging was too light and had torque problems, so it prevented Tiger from making the most exacting swing possible, which has always been his goal.

Tiger still has not made the switch to steel. However, he is now more of a power-control player off the tee, thanks to a new forty-five-inch-long Nike Ignite, 460-cubic-centimeter driver featuring 8.5 degrees of loft, and the changes Haney helped Tiger make to his setup and swing, starting with the takeaway action.

Once Tiger settles into a correct setup position, he swings his arms back very quietly, with the club moving slightly outside the target line, at least at the start of the swing, while the right knee stays flexed.

Under Anselmo, Tiger straightened his right knee while taking the club back, which is something Anselmo and his friend Mike Austin advocate. Presently, under Haney, Tiger keeps his right knee bent slightly and firmly braced. This new positive feature of Tiger's swing puts a governor on hip turn, and it prevents Tiger from spinning out and/or turning his hips so vigorously that power is drained from his swing.

By restricting the turning action of the hips while turning the shoulders, Tiger is able to direct the club upward, instead of extending it back on a wide arc, and he creates resistance between the upper and lower body, a key to Ben Hogan's power.

What triggers Tiger's good swinging action is an out-in-up takeaway action, shown here in the accompanying two photographs (above, left; above, right).

"Some prominent golfers advocate taking a big turn with the hips," said Ben Hogan in his classic instruction book, *Five Lessons: The Modern Fundamentals of Golf*.

"I don't go along with this. A golfer wants to have this tension; he wants the midsection of his body to be tightened up, for this tension is the key to the whole downswing."

Jim McLean, one of the *Golf Digest* teaching professionals, explored the value of building resistance in the swing in more depth and, after years of conducting intense research with pro Mike McTeigue, was able to prove that players who turn their shoulders far more than their hips hit the ball longer. So, everything you have ever heard about turning the hips and shoulders as much as is comfortably possible during the backswing is malarkey.

"After studying the pros, I can tell you for sure that one secret to generating high club head speed and creating power in the swing is to create a gap—the bigger the better—between the shoulder and hip turn," McLean told me.

Since taking lessons from Haney, it's apparent to me and other swing connoisseurs, such as Geoff Bryant, president of the United States Golf Teachers Federation, that Tiger's sequencing is better than ever before.

"Because the movement of Tiger's swing is in the ideal order—back muscles, arms, shoulders, hips, hands, and finally the swinging club—the tempo, timing, and rhythm of his backswing is superb," said Bryant.

As Tiger's arms come into play, the club moves back low to the ground and slightly outside the target line in the initial stage of the swing, giving him all the width he needs to create a powerful swing arc. Once the shoulders start turning and squaring up, due to his new and improved open alignment setup, the left arm moves upward and matches the plane of the club—again, more upright in nature. Beyond question, this is one of Tiger's secrets. Prior to taking lessons from Haney, Tiger often set up with his feet closed to the target line and his shoulders open. This setup, particularly his closed stance, opened up a passageway for him to swing the club back on a flat plane, as Butch Harmon preferred. The trouble was, Tiger's swing got flatter and flatter, and eventually led to his slump of hitting enough off-line shots to keep him out of the winner's circle in major championships.

Presently, Tiger also keeps his right hip locked until weight "loads" into his right foot and leg. This lock-and-load action of the right hip is another one of Tiger's secrets that allows him to keep the club on the correct path and upright plane. Before going to Haney, Tiger coiled his right hip too soon and too much in a rotating fashion. Again, this fault caused him to swing on an overly flat plane and in turn played havoc with his ability to time the downswing and square the club's face at impact. Now Tiger locks and loads the right hip, then even shifts it slightly laterally before turning it, to protect against swinging on a flat plane.

Jim McLean, who I've worked with on instruction articles while senior editor of *Golf Magazine*, was the first to notice this feature of Tiger's new swing, and said this recently: "This is one move that will help Tiger hit the ball even further and more accurately, and if Haney's responsible for this move he deserves a lot of credit." McLean makes this strong statement knowing that a combined lateral and rotational hip turn on the backswing, rather than solely a turning action or a slide, is necessary to properly loading the right side. In fact, McLean's told me on several occasions that this type action (similar to Tiger's) is what allows the body's center to move slightly away from the target on the backswing. That's a good thing because, as a re-

Tiger's right hip only starts coiling, albeit minimally, once weight begins loading into his right foot and leg.

sult of the center moving the weight starts to shift to a right-handed player's right foot and leg, and the arms, hands, and club move freely back, with the club also tracking on a path that's never too far inside. Moving the club back to the inside is what one of my favorite teachers Jim Flick calls the "danger zone," and that's the place Tiger ended up in during his bad patch.

The other plus factor of Tiger's new hip action is that it allows him to increase his power gap, because he now also turns his shoulders even more fully, achieving strong resistance between the upper and lower body. Working the big muscles of the shoulders is very vital to starting the club back smoothly. It's only when you start using the hands to control the takeaway that your tempo quickens. So that by the time you reach the impact zone, you actually decelerate and end up losing distance off the tee, which is exactly what happened to Tiger during one stage of his winless streak in the major championships.

In taking the club back, Tiger gently starts turning his left hand in a clockwise direction so that, by the time both his hands pass his right leg and he begins hinging his right wrist, the back of his left hand and the palm of his right are parallel to the target line, or set exactly in the position all of you should strive for when reaching the top of the swing. This turn and set move, as opposed to trying to keep the back of the left hand facing the target at the beginning of the takeaway and the wrist locked all the way to waist height, is an element of Tiger's new backswing that now allows him to consistently keep the club on plane and arrive in the same solid position at the top of the swing.

I hope I have convinced you to stop trying to keep the back of the left hand square to the target longer in the takeaway. If not, let me repeat the words of Severiano Ballesteros, one of golf's all-time smoothest, yet powerful swingers. "Seve" relayed this instructional message to me

TIGER'S TURBO-DRIVE SWING: CAUGHT ON CAMERA

The most glaring feature of Tiger's new setup position, designed to promote a supercontrolled, superpowerful fade shot off the tee, is the open
alignment of his feet and body. Look closely at how Tiger's feet and
shoulders point left of where the club's face is aimed. Jack Nicklaus won
eighteen major championships setting up in a similar fashion to Tiger.
There's no doubt that an open setup position gives you a better visual
picture of the intended flight line and allows you to make a free swing.

Tiger now starts the club back outside the target line, but parallel to the open alignment lines established by his feet and body, in order to further promote a type of swing that will produce a powerfully hit Turbo-Drive fade shot. In order to groove the correct start-back position of the club, do what top teacher Don Trahan told his son, PGA Tour player D. J. Trahan, to do when he was learning the game: imagine you are trying to push the clubhead back into a baseball catcher's mitt.

What's so unique about this new takeaway action is that the club swings out and up, while Tiger's right shoulder turns into a dead square position and his right hip remains locked in position. Former Masters champion and power hitter Fred Couples looks very similar in the takeaway, proving that you don't need to extend the club straight back and create width early on in the swing to hit the ball hard.

This is another new magical move of Tiger's that can be traced back to his setup position. Because Tiger now starts from open address, his arms direct the club on an upright plane rather than well inside the target line. One of my favorite teachers, Jim Flick, calls the area behind the golfer the "danger zone," because when the club swings back on an overly flat plane it requires you to make at least one major compensatory move to return the club to a square impact position.

Tiger now swings the club into the ideal at the top position, with the clubshaft parallel to the line the ball will start flying on, and creates power by turning his shoulders far more than his hips. According to Jim McLean, the bigger the gap or differential between the shoulder turn and hip turn—what he calls the "X-Factor"—the more torque there is between your upper and lower body. In the impact zone, this torque promotes an increase in clubhead speed and, in turn, higher ball speed and added distance off the tee.

Hank Haney and Tiger Woods have teamed well, mixing talents in the search for the perfect swing, and this on-plane drop down move (left), marked by an exaggerated hinge of the right wrist (right), is living proof of a swing secret caught on camera. Johnny Miller, a legendary solid ball striker, was known for holding the angle, but even his position did not match Tiger's. Tiger's right-wrist hinge angle is so severe and evident in his new swing that I am baffled as to why top teacher Mike Malaska made this statement in a July 2005 *Golf Magazine* article entitled "Tigerize Your Drives": "Contrary to conventional wisdom, Tiger does not delay the unhinging of his wrists for as long as possible."

One chief reason why Tiger's control off the tee has reached such a high performance level is his improved footwork, proven by this photograph showing him keeping the left foot planted and letting the heel of the right foot lead the toe end of the right foot. Tiger's right foot move matches that of Ben Hogan, one of the game's all-time most accurate golfers. This is obviously no coincidence, considering that Hank Haney, Tiger's new teacher, studied Hogan's swing.

Tiger's firm left leg—turned-in right knee, vertical right-foot position—and relaxed finish prove that he employed a free and fluid body-club action.

It seems Tiger is back doing what his longtime coach John Anselmo always stressed he should do: swing through his body, not through his hands, with the downswing goal to end up balanced on his left foot and leg.

when we worked on the book *Natural Golf,* at a time when he was driving the ball superbly.

"The typical club player trying to employ an ultra-square takeaway frequently makes one grave error that ultimately causes the ball to slice. Most commonly, he resists the natural tendency for the wrists to hinge, thus becoming so stiff-armed that his hands can't release effectively in the hitting area, with the result that the club's face arrives at the ball both weakly and open aligned right of target."

Sound familiar? Of course it does. Tiger had this problem because I believe he strived too hard to create power by extending the arms and club back with locked wrists, rather than by properly turning his hips and shoulders the right degree.

It's a different story now. Once Tiger's left arm is parallel to the target line at around hip height, he hinges his right wrist and the club then starts moving upward, rather than inside, with his right elbow staying closer to his body and pointing directly downward, rather than "flying" and pointing outward. All these new keys help him swing on plane, a lot like Ben Hogan, and set him in the ideal position to swing the club down on the proper path and plane. I am now convinced, after seeing Tiger's driving game improve, that you will hit more powerfully accurate shots if you keep the right elbow relatively close to your right side.

"Winging the right elbow far away from the body indicates that your arms are overcontrolling the action," said teaching guru Phil Ritson.

Granted, the arms play a vital role in the takeaway, but once the club reaches the parallel point at the end of the takeaway, the desired upward swinging action of the club should be controlled by the hinging of your right wrist and turning the left shoulder under your chin, while keeping your upper left arm glued to your chest.

Before going to Haney, Tiger used to turn his left knee outward toward the ball, which is a move that automatically caused the right hip to overcoil and the club, ultimately, to swing too far inside. Now, Tiger's left knee moves inward, which helps control his hip turn and causes weight to shift correctly to the inside of his right foot and leg, instead of to his right heel or even the outside of his right foot.

Once the weight shift commences, Tiger starts rotating his right hip, although because he started from an open alignment position rather than square, it does not rotate quite so far around as before. Therefore, the club swings more up than around, another element of his swing that has changed him for the better while taking lessons from Haney.

As Tiger continues to swing back, into a braced right leg, resistance and powerful torque are already starting to be created. The more torque you build into your swing on the backswing, the more powerful your downswing.

As Tiger continues swinging the arms back and turning his left shoulder more fully under his chin, the club moves further upward, but not on a steep plane, because the turning right shoulder flattens the plane, out just enough.

At this stage of the swing, when the club is moving closer to the top, Tiger no longer has to really worry about his elbow flying like it did during his slump, as long as the plane of the left shoulder matches the plane of the club, more upright in nature than flat.

If you have been playing this game for a long time, you might have heard that it is okay to let the right elbow fly, namely because players such as John Daly, Jack Nicklaus, and Fred Couples do, and they hit the ball fine. It's true that this trio do hit the ball powerfully. However, you must understand that these great golfers have played golf this way all their lives and have grown accustomed to making compensations during the swing to get the club back on plane and return the club's face to a square position at impact.

There are also some teachers who believe the flying right elbow position is more natural. That may be true if what they claim is more natural feels better. The fact is, in golf what often feels good is not good for your game.

Feeling as if the left shoulder is rocking downward (not dipping), rather than rotating clockwise, hinging the right wrist early in the backswing, and swinging fully back to parallel, or with the club shaft slightly laid off or pointing left as Tiger often does, will ensure that the right elbow stays fairly close to your body and the club swings more up than around. There is no doubt that the shorter, three-quarter-length swing that Butch Harmon advocated allowed Tiger to better control his distance with his short irons. However, there is also no doubt that striving for this position with the driver caused his right elbow to fly and did damage to his tee-shot game. Your lesson: Make as full a backswing as possible with your driver, while feeling balanced and in control and, of course, keeping your right elbow close to your right side.

I've argued this point with some teachers, such as Don Trahan, who advocate a three-quarter backswing, and others who still think Tiger is employing a three-quarter action because they have only watched him hit drives during a golf tournament, when following him around the course. As strange as this may sound, you can't learn much that way, because it's hard for the naked eye to pick up Tiger's precise positions. It's difficult to determine exactly how far Tiger swings back, because before you know it he's swinging down again, only taking one-fifth of a second to swing from the top to the ball. So some teachers just assume Tiger is still making a three-quarter action when driving, and then they recommend this compact swing to their students. Other teachers recommend a full-swing drive but a three-quarter action to students looking to learn how to enhance their control with short or medium irons and get the ball to stop more quickly by hitting a fade shot. I have no problem with this iron-play swing strategy, as long as you follow Tiger's example of setting up open and keep your right elbow pointing directly downward when reaching the three-quarter point in the backswing. I say that knowing

If you are looking to hit a super-controlled, soft-landing fade shot with a short or medium iron, follow Tiger's example of setting up open and employing a three-quarter backswing (top photos). When looking to hit dead-straight iron shots into a strong headwind, set up square and employ a fairly full backswing (bottom photos).

that if you let the right elbow fly, your swing is likely to get too steep and cause you to hit the ball fat or hit shots that fly fast off the club's face and finish up approximately twenty yards over the green. Incidentally, while on the subject of hitting irons, for those of you who sometimes like to hit dead straight "darts" into a headwind, I recommend you follow Tiger's example of setting up square and making a full backswing.

All you have to do to see what's right and what's wrong is look at the wonderful photographs contained in this book's color insert. These photographs reveal Tiger's most critical backswing positions, so you can learn a lot about correct golf technique by studying them; but, to clear up any confusion, look most closely at the photograph showing Tiger at the top of his driver swing. You'll see that he swings the club back fully to the top.

Tiger is able to swing more fully now when playing a driver, simply because he no longer strives for the three-quarter position. Also, his shoulders and upper torso are turning more than ever before, and this powerful coiling action is responsible for his newly found power. Most recently, at the 2005 U.S. Open, Tiger led the driving statistics list, averaging 320 yards off the tee. Furthermore, en route to winning the 2005 British open, Tiger made a habit of driving par-4 holes and hitting par 5s with a driver and an iron.

"Haney is a very good all-around teacher, who is known for being able to increase a player's driving distance," said Jim McLean.

When fully wound up at the top, have someone, such as a parent or local pro, check your positions. Alternatively, have your swing filmed so that you can sit back and review it. Tiger looks at film of his swing, so why shouldn't you?

To review what you want to look for at the top, use these guidelines:

1. Your left wrist should be flat. (This will ensure that the club stays square).

2. The club should be parallel to the ball's initial flight line when hitting a fade, and parallel to the target line when hitting a straight shot. (Striving for either one of these positions will encourage a powerful turn.)

3. Your right elbow should be pointing downward toward the ground. (This position will ensure that the club stays on the ideal upright plane, like Tiger's.)

4. The majority of your lower body weight should be loaded into your right instep and right leg. (This position confirms that you have made a full turn-and-shift action but have not swayed your body too far away from the target.)

5. Both your shoulders should have turned at least ninety degrees, while your hips only forty-five. (Turning the shoulders more than the hips builds resistance between the upper and lower body, and this torque translates to added clubhead speed and power at impact.)

6. Your right knee should be flexed, rather than straight. (Keeping the right knee flexed allows you to build a brace to coil against and encourages you to push the club upward, rather than around your body on a flat plane.)

7. Your back should face the target. (This position indicates a full, free coiling action of the body that's needed to further create power—power that will be unleashed on the downswing.)

8. Both elbows should be virtually level, even with one another. So that, if you draw a line from one to the other, that line together with your forearms would form a perfect triangle that looks straight rather than tilted. (Check this position by having your swing photographed or videotaped from the down-target angle, because it indicates that the backswing is perfect. Look at the photograph of Tiger at the top of the backswing and you will see a window of air inside the triangle I just spoke about. That's what you want to see.)

By pointing out all of Tiger's backswing revisions and brand-new positions, you can see that he is on a mission. Hogan and Nicklaus were also always on a mission, looking to play better golf, even after they had shot great scores to win a major championship. As good as these two players were, though, they did not ever learn to arrive in as perfect a position at the top of the backswing as Tiger does today. Hank Haney and Tiger deserve a lot of credit for the work

When hitting a Turbo-Drive fade, you can see that Tiger employs a full backswing, with the clubshaft slightly "laid off" yet parallel to the line the ball will start traveling along.

they've done and the courage they showed in accomplishing their goals.

So, there's been a method to his madness all the time the critics questioned Tiger's plans. I hope you now understand his backswing enough to incorporate at least some of his innovative movements into your own swing. If not, keep practicing, and freezing each new position until you can groove each one, then let them flow together as smoothly as a piece by Mozart, into one uninterrupted, fluid motion. Once you do, you can start learning how to swing down like Tiger, by carefully reading the instructions and looking at the photographs that follow in the upcoming chapter.

4. DOWN TIME

Correctly timing the downswing is all about coordinating
the movement of the body with the movement of the club
while generating power centers and holding the angle in
the right wrist until impact.

I n explaining Tiger's new downswing action, I'm going
to describe how Tiger's body moves while he makes the
transition, from the top of the backswing into the hitting area, then straightens his hinged right wrist in the impact zone, driving the club hard into the golf ball.

In order to emulate Tiger's unique downswing, it's
necessary that you fully understand where you are sup-
posed to be when completing the backswing, and that you
appreciate that it only takes approximately one fifth of a
second to swing into the ball from that point at the top.
Furthermore, you must have a vivid picture in your mind
of the through-impact and finish positions you are trying
to swing into. I'm emphatic about this point, and am frustrated by golf professionals and teachers who give the im-

When you reach the top of the backswing (above), it's a good idea to have a vivid mental image of Tiger's early follow-through, late follow-through, and finish positions, highlighted in the three photographs on the facing page.

pression that the downswing is totally a reflexive action. That's wrong. The body does not spring back automatically once you reach the top of the backswing, no matter what has been written in best-selling instruction books.

"I'm so stretched and coiled at the top that I'm literally

forced to react and start down," said Nicklaus in his book *Golf My Way.*

"The muscles in the upper left side of the back are stretched to a point of tautness, wound so intensely that you cannot hold them in that position at the top of the backswing," said Carl Lohren, the author of *One Move to Better Golf*.

Nicklaus, Lohren, and other golfing gurus are certainly correct to declare that the downswing happens so quickly, in a flash basically, that it cannot be consciously directed. However, it's wrong for any golfer who understands the swing, and has studied great players like Tiger Woods, to ignore the fact that each and every golfer needs a boost physically, such as a lateral push with the hips, to start the downswing. Top tour professionals, including Tiger, pause at the top of the backswing for only a moment, except Kenny Perry and Jay Haas, who practically come to a full stop. Therefore, it is logical to conclude that each and every player must depend on a singular downswing trigger or minimove, albeit one that is directed by the subconscious mind ideally, and that allows weight to shift from the right side to the left side, and for the arms, hands, and club to start moving in the opposite direction, toward the target.

What I find so fascinating about downswing triggers is that there have been so many recommended by teachers in books and magazine articles, or from pro golfers conducting clinics on The Golf Channel. One recommends you clear your left hip first, while others recommend that you pull the club down with your hands, replant your left foot, or rotate your right hip counterclockwise. It's no wonder that average golfers like you are confused when it comes to understanding correct downswing mechanics. There is just so much

The intense expression on Tiger's face proves that you don't simply spring back after reaching the top of the swing. Starting down requires a physical trigger.

information being offered that the typical club-level player may just as well pick a golf tip out of a hat and try it. Well, relax, because I'm going to clear up the confusion by giving you feedback on the downswing, based on studying the best new swing on tour that is employed by Tiger Woods, unquestionably the greatest player of the twenty-first century.

No two players swing exactly the same. Yet, once you reach the top like Tiger, with your shoulders turned at least twice as much as your hips, with most of your body weight on the inside of your right foot and leg, your right knee flexed and braced, left wrist flat, the club's face square, and the clubshaft parallel to the target line, or slightly "laid off" and pointing slightly left, you should do what my research shows Tiger does: trigger the downswing by shifting the hips laterally, while practically simultaneously replanting your left foot (or putting pressure on it, if you are flexible enough to have kept it planted firmly on the ground during the backswing). The chief reason this type of trigger is so vitally important is that it gives your hands, arms, and club time to catch up with your lower body. If you follow the advice given by many of today's teachers, who say you should rotate your left hip counterclockwise the split second you reach the top, the body will get so far out in front of the club that the club's face will come into impact open rather than square to the ball, and the shot will fly right of target. Alternatively, you will sense that your timing is off and feel so blocked by your body that you will likely flip your right hand over your left hand, or vigorously rotate your right forearm over your left forearm, to try and save an inevitable bad shot by attempting to square the club's face. The trouble is, most often those who do employ either of these bailout moves end up closing the clubface and hitting a hook. Before going to Haney for lessons, Tiger was experiencing both of these problems. Now that he is not, don't think for a second that Haney simply gave Tiger a few simple instructions and Tiger stood up to the ball and hit it superbly.

These two photographs, shot from two different angles, illustrate Tiger's lateral hip-shift downswing trigger—a move that precedes the clearing action of the hips.

Golfers who understand the game of golf know full well that whenever you make even a small change to your setup, backswing, or downswing, it takes time to get back on track. That's why the critics had no business "bugging" Tiger about the slow progress he was making before he started winning again in 2005.

Since you are looking to improve your game, you must appreciate that any downswing trigger you want to incorporate into your swing requires conscious thought—at first anyway—when you are first learning how to employ it. Any downswing trigger only becomes second nature and gets controlled by the subconscious mind after you rehearse it over and over in practice and ingrain it through drill work. Until that happens, expect to go through bad patches and even be prepared to play worse before you play better. I'm telling you this so you don't give up right away and revert back to your old swing and make no progress at all.

The other downswing problem Tiger had, that was addressed first by his previous teacher Butch Harmon, was pushing off his right foot at the start of the downswing. The average player making this very same mistake would have absolutely no chance of being able to recover and hit a good shot. Tiger, however, has such great eye-hand coordination and such exceptional feel for the moving club, that he could often hit the ball quite well with this fault ingrained into his technique. Why? He had learned to make compensations, but did not even know it. And then one day all hell broke loose and he could not find his game, so Butch went to work.

Butch informed Tiger straight out that spinning his hips counterclockwise at the start of the downswing and swinging too fast were causing his overactive right-foot problems, which led to a loss of balance and off-line shots. To remedy this problem, Butch told me that he tamed Tiger by having him swing at 75 percent of his full speed, and he further enhanced his control by having him hit flat-footed shots.

After a period of lessons, in 1996 Butch told me that Tiger had improved his foot problem, but not as much with the driver as with the irons. Unfortunately, Tiger had not fully remedied the problem and had paid the price. Fortunately, Tiger was able to hit enough good shots, because Butch encouraged him to do what Ben Hogan had done—stop clearing the left hip so fast at the start of the downswing and trigger the downward motion with a bump of the left hip. The trouble was, Tiger never did quite develop enough of a hip slide, just as he had not quite fixed his right-foot problem. Therefore, although he won tournaments around the world under Harmon, due mostly to an uncanny ability to hit great recovery shots and super pitches, chips, and putts, he never developed into a super-consistent driver of the ball. Sure, Tiger had golden patches where he hit the ball far and straight, often like a machine in fact, but sooner or later what was bound to happen happened. He lost his great timing and, as a result, he could no longer make those same compensatory moves he once made in order to "cover up" for a fault.

Since taking lessons from Haney, Tiger has greatly improved his timing, doing something the supersteady driver of the ball, Ben Hogan, did practically at the same time he shifted his hips laterally at the start of the downswing. This is something Hogan never wrote about or talked about, but a key I discovered when examining sequence photographs of Hogan's driver swing, taken by the late legendary photographer Chuck Brenkus.

Like Hogan, Tiger now pushes the instep of his right foot downward into the turf, with the heel of the shoe moving toward the target ahead of the toe end. This one move now grounds Tiger and allows him to be poised to make a much more balanced and powerful downswing. In my mind, this truly is one of Tiger's new downswing secrets.

Under Haney, Tiger's swing is the best it has ever been, yet Tiger admits the process takes time. That's his way, I think, of telling the golf world he can even get better. Whether he does get even better only time will tell, but for now he is the best model for any golfer looking to reach their full potential as a power player.

One chief reason why Tiger's downswing no longer

At this point in the swing, when Tiger's club drops into the perfect hitting slot, the heel of Tiger's shoe leads its toe end (below, left) and his hips begin clearing, albeit not yet vigorously (below, right).

TIGER'S NEW SWING

looks forced is that, once he shifts his hips laterally, his right elbow drops into his side, directing the club automatically into the perfect hitting slot. At this point in the swing, Tiger's hips start uncoiling.

The downswing is all about coordinating the timing sequence of the body with the golf club, and I cannot stress how important it is to let the hips slide laterally, in order that the club ultimately fall into the ideal hitting position and remain on plane all the way to impact.

One of the most common faults made by amateur golfers, and one you have probably experienced yourself, is jutting the right shoulder outward at the start of the downswing—a fault that causes the club to move off plane and swing across the target line, rather than along it, through impact. The result: a pull-slice shot. You can cure this problem by letting the lower body take charge of the downswing, starting by moving the hips laterally first, then clearing them in a counterclockwise direction.

Once weight shifts to Tiger's left foot and leg, and the club drops down parallel to the plane line—and inside it, as Haney believes is best, and ideally on a shallower arc— Tiger rotates his left hip so vigorously to the left that his clubhead speed starts increasing at a rapid rate. At this point in the swing, energy starts moving down Tiger's arms and into his hands, with multiplying power steadily being transferred down the clubshaft. Eventually, this power will be sent into the clubhead, with Tiger's club speed reaching 130 miles per hour and the snap of the clubshaft slapping

Once weight shifts more fully to Tiger's left foot and leg, Tiger's left hip starts clearing at a rapid rate of speed (above, left), and even faster still, as the club works its way into impact (above, right).

the club's face solidly into the ball. However, you are not at that point yet. Let's see what Tiger does next.

To complete the job of making a full-body release and swinging the club into the hitting area, Tiger must bring his right side into play. The right hip and knee must rotate counterclockwise to open a "door" for the club to move freely through and swing back to a square position at impact.

"When Tiger is really on, he generates incredible speed and power by increasing what I call the 'X-factor' differential on the downswing—the gap between the shoulders and hips," said world renowned golf instructor Jim McLean.

"The ideal way to make this happen is to rotate the hips while holding the shoulders back and delaying the release of the club; but the motion must be smooth, synchronized, timed."

Prior to taking lessons from Hank Haney, Tiger had problems employing the proper downswing moves and increasing his gap. Because he set up with his feet closed and tended to swing the club back on too flat a path and plane, the club had to travel farther and come from well inside the target line on the way down. However, since he's been taking lessons from Haney, I've noticed that Tiger's open stance presets his hips in essentially a cleared position, so that he is less compelled to quicken his tempo on the downswing. Tiger's initial lateral hip shift action, together with his new right foot push down move, allows his hands, arms, and the club to drop down on the perfect plane, alleviating the need to manipulate the club to square it up to the ball at impact. These changes have definitely allowed Tiger to drive the ball farther and, more importantly, more accurately.

When observing Tiger, I've also noticed that the split second he shifts his left knee toward the target, his legs separate a little farther apart. This "leg separation" is reminiscent of golfing great Sam Snead, and serves as a catalyst in creating powerful leverage on the downswing. The toward-the-target action of Tiger's left knee lets the entire left side play the lead role on the downswing, as it should, according to the game's top teachers and pros on the PGA, LPGA, Champions, and Nike tours.

Once the left side takes control, rotating away from the target, with weight shifting to the outside of the left foot, the right side of Tiger's body comes into play. In turn, the speed of his Nike 460-cubic-centimeter driver keeps increasing as it heads toward impact.

In the past, another one of Tiger's swing faults was an overactive right side. Although I consider it natural for a right-handed golfer to let the right side take control of the downswing, I also understand that a good golf swing does not operate according to the laws of nature, and a golfer cannot swing according to the "if it feels good, do it" philosophy. Golf has been called a game of opposites, and one reason why this is so is because a right-handed player must get used to letting his left side control the downswing action.

Allowing the right side to dominate the start of the downswing disrupts the timing of your swing and plays havoc with the direction of your shots. Once you employ a faulty downswing action, hitting the ball with your right hand, arm, and shoulder, the club is thrown off the correct path and plane. Depending on how you compensate, you are much more likely to hit anything but an accurate shot.

Tiger's pre-Haney, right-sided, controlled downswing was caused by pushing off his right foot at the start of the downswing. Now, by retaining pressure in his right knee and the instep of his right foot until the club drops into the ideal hitting slot, as well as keeping his body more centered due to the leg separation I talked about earlier, Tiger's left side plays the lead role and, ironically, pulls the right side through the ball.

"It's been proven scientifically that any pulling action on an object, in this case the body, is better and stronger than a pushing action," said one of golf's finest instructors and players, Australian Peter Croker.

Maintaining his "center," albeit for only a split second, gives Tiger's arms, hands, and club, time to catch up with his leading lower body, once he moves through the slot position toward impact. It's obvious from Tiger's play that because of better timing he no longer feels the urge to manipulate the club to get it back on plane. Instead, he now swings the club with much more freedom and control, due to keeping his upper left arm fairly close to his chest in the hitting area. This same tip will prevent you from throwing the club outside the target line and hitting a pull-slice shot.

In following my analysis of Tiger's downswing, and looking at the photographs contained within this chapter and the color insert, I want you to remember this one, critical instructional dogma when practicing or playing: *The lateral slide of the hips, combined with the clearing action of the hips, along with the resulting weight shift and pulling force, automatically brings the club into impact.*

Having collaborated on the book *Total Shotmaking* with Fred Couples, one of golf's longest-ball hitters, I found it intriguing that there are similarities between the downswing he employs and the one Tiger learned from his former teachers and now Hank Haney. It's worth sharing Fred's ideas on the swing, since they will serve as a prerequisite to learning and appreciating Tiger's magical moves that, again, are similar to Fred's shift, drop, and release, downswing actions.

As Fred explained to me, the shift refers to the transfer of weight from the right side to the left side and is the result of proper hip action. The drop relates to the right arm and club falling into the slot. The release refers to the coordinated relationship between the shift and rotation of his body and the whiplike motion of his arms and wrists.

"At times, my reactions are so good that I feel I can snap the clubhead off the end of the clubshaft through the impact area with my aggressive releasing motion, and it's ironic that under pressure it's this free releasing action that I rely on to hit accurate, strong shots," said Couples. The main reason Tiger hits the ball so long is that his release action is even better than those employed by Couples and other PGA Tour players.

No release in golf is more powerful than Tiger's, and that's because the clearing action of his hips is so forceful, yet so fluid now that the speed of his arms, hands, and club, steadily increase in the hit zone, especially at impact, when he finally unhinges his right wrist. Wow! This one, seemingly simple move, involving the right wrist, is responsible for Tiger's clubhead speed reaching a crescendo at impact, and his ability to wallop the Nike One Platinum ball he prefers to play with high into the air. But we have not reached impact yet. The club is still moving downward, having passed the point when it was parallel to the ground and perfectly on plane, coming closer to the point where it meets the ball.

Because the downswing happens so quickly, Tiger's downswing works on automatic pilot, meaning he has no time to think about what he's doing. You can only reach this advanced stage of letting go and letting the swing just happen if you learn and groove each vital move through purposeful practice sessions.

If you set up like Tiger, plus swing the club back on a circular-shaped plane, with your left arm moving up under your left shoulder, just like Tiger—and robots used for testing golf equipment—you are likely to swing down with your shoulders, arms, hands, and club moving correctly in the opposite direction. On the other hand, if you set up incorrectly, then feel that your body or the club is out of position at the top of the backswing, you are likely to hit a bad shot, simply because the downswing happens so fast that it is virtually impossible to make a correction.

What keeps the club moving toward the ball is the momentum generated by a free and fluid hip-clearing action, and a good degree of arm speed, enough to swing at least eighty miles per hour. Once your right side follows your rotating left side, the club will whip powerfully into the ball.

Tiger generates so much power and hits drives so hard

now because he also keeps his upper body weight leaning away from the target, while bracing his left side and hitting powerfully *up* on the ball, much like a world-class fighter landing an extra-strong uppercut punch. The main reason Tiger's drives now fly higher and carry so far in the air, other than the new elements related to his setup and backswing, is that he creates a bigger angle between his right wrist and forearm. Once the wrist straightens, precisely at the moment of impact, and he releases through the shot, power is maximized. All he has to do is release the club normally, with the right forearm turning over slightly, to deliver the club squarely into the ball and hit a dead-straight drive. To hit a power fade, all Tiger or any of you have to do is hold on more firmly with the left hand, so the snap-back, rehinge action of the right wrist is delayed, and you get the feeling of turning your right hand under your left in the impact zone, with the club's face coming into the ball square to your final landing spot, yet slightly open to the initial flight line of the ball.

Nowadays, when Tiger hits his bread-and-butter, highly controlled power fade drive, the ball shoots high into the air, then levels off into a forceful, penetrating flight trajectory, as it works its way from slightly left of target into a bull's-eye area of fairway some three hundred yards from the tee.

Just as it's easier to find your way to a particular destination with a road map, as opposed to "winging it," it's easier to swing into impact like Tiger if you have a good visual image of yourself in the correct impact position. For this reason, let me point out the unique qualities of Tiger's hitting position, so that you give yourself the best possible chance of matching it. To be honest, since Tiger is blessed with so many innate physical attributes, almost all of you will never match Tiger's power. However, make no mistake, if you can match his swing positions by reading my instructions, you will likely come to understand the instructional message and stand a darn good chance of hitting the ball longer than ever before.

Tiger's superfluid, supercoordinated, right-sided body-club release is why he is able to whip the club through in a flash (below, left) and hit the ball so hard (below, right).

As Tiger nears impact, his upper body tilts away from the target, while his left hip clears to the left and his right hip drives more forward, then around. Tiger's left hip and left shoulder are much higher than his right hip and shoulder, as he prepares to hit against a firmly braced left leg.

Rotating his right hip and knee toward the target with such thrust that his right heel is pulled off the ground, together with that rehinge, snap-back action of the right wrist I referred to earlier, is what allows Tiger to make such powerful contact with the ball.

Since taking lessons from Haney, Tiger's left arm and club form a virtual straight line at impact, and his balance is superb, too—which explains why all the dots of his swing connect correctly, and why he's now able to hit the ball much more accurately with the driver.

There are some golf instructors who see no point in teaching the correct follow-through and finish positions of the downswing, arguing that if the student sets up in the right manner, arrives in a good position at the top of the backswing, and swings the club down on plane, he or she will swing into the ideal follow-through and finish positions. I don't agree. I argue that if a golfer has a vivid visual picture in his mind's eye of what a good, Tigerlike follow-through and finish look like, he or she will be less likely to hit at the ball and, instead, be more likely to swing back and down correctly, generate maximum clubhead speed in the impact zone, and hit powerfully through the ball.

"Although the ball has already been hit, the follow-

Here's Tiger in the follow-through and finish positions when hitting a driver (top, left; top, right) and when hitting a medium iron (bottom, left; bottom, right).

through and finish are important parts of your golf swing," said Hank Haney in his book *The Only Golf Lesson You'll Ever Need.*

"You might work from the start of your swing to the finish most of the time, but you can do the opposite and still achieve some great results. A thought, feeling, or image of your finish position can often change your entire swing."

Having made my argument for knowing the elements of a good follow-through and finish, I'll now discuss the specific movements involved.

In order to match Tiger in the earlier follow-through position, ideally you want:

1. Your left shoulder pointing at the sky, your right shoulder angled toward the ground.

2. Your arms in front of your body.

3. Your left palm and the back of your right hand facing the target line, in a "dead square" position.

4. Your left leg virtually straight, with little or no flex in the knee.

5. Your right knee bowed inward.

6. Your right shoe's heel dramatically ahead of its toe end.

7. Your body weight heavily on your left foot and leg.

8. You chin pointing at the spot where the ball was before being struck, and your eyes focused on that very same spot.

9. Your left hip pocket turned far enough left, so as not to be visible when viewed from either the face-on or down-target angle.

10. Your right hip pocket dead square to the target line.

11. The head of the club pointing directly at your target.

To match Tiger's finish position, ideally you want:

1: Your belt buckle facing the target.

2. Ninety percent of your weight balanced on the outside of your left heel and the remainder balanced on the toe end of your right foot.

3. Both your arms folded at the elbow.

4. Your hands positioned level with the back of your neck and behind your right ear.

5. The club shaft to be angled outward toward the spot where the ball was before it was struck.

6. Your left leg straight, with virtually no flex in the left knee.

7. Your right leg turned well inward and touching your left leg.

8. Your right shoulder slightly higher than your left.

9. Your eyes looking down the target line.

10. To be balanced and experience the sensation of having made an effortless driver-swing.

Of course, unlike Tiger you do not have Hank Haney as your coach to check these positions and watch the flight of the ball to spot any inconsistent patterns. That's okay; see your local golf professional for a lesson, or view video-tape taken of your swing, until what you see on camera strongly resembles the follow-through and finish positions of Tiger Woods contained in this book.

Tiger's caddy, Steve Williams, and his coach, Hank Haney, are always watching and thinking when Tiger's hitting shots, since Tiger is a golfer who likes to receive feedback after a practice session or round of golf.

5. THERE'S ONLY ROOM FOR IMPROVEMENT

In the search for the perfect swing, even a player like Tiger Woods has had to learn from his mistakes and groove good habits through drill work on the practice tee.

One common thread between Tiger Woods and all power hitters on the PGA Tour is a passion for practice. Tiger spends hours on the practice tee at Isleworth Country Club in Orlando, Florida, where he resides, and hits balls before and after tournament rounds, often with coach Hank Haney advising him. Haney also often follows Tiger around the course during practice rounds, obviously checking Tiger's swing positions and shot-making strategies.

If you are like the majority of country club golfers, hearing the word "practice" is like hearing the word "dentist," especially if you know you've got a problem in your swing that is going to require a few hours of hard work on the driving range to solve.

To be honest, I never liked the idea of practical practice. I loved to hit buckets of balls with the driver, figuring that if I went through enough buckets, eventually my swing would get better or return to its old good form. Wrong!

During my sixteen-year stint as senior editor of instruction at *Golf Magazine,* I learned quickly from the top teachers and tour pros I worked with on articles that true, valuable practice revolves around working on specific movements that are designed to help you build a good swing that will repeat and produce powerful on-target shots.

Of course, I've been even more fortunate to have talked to Tiger's first teacher Rudy Duran and his present professional teacher Hank Haney, and to have worked on books with two of Tiger's former teachers, John Anselmo and Butch Harmon. I also converse with top teachers regularly, like Jim McLean, who keeps his finger on the pulse of what's going on in the golf world more than any other teacher in the business. Jim often shares with me something new he's heard or witnessed regarding swing technique, such as a drill he saw a player working on. In fact, Jim recently described to me a practice drill he saw Hank Haney teaching Tiger on the West Coast that was instrumental in the development of his new swing. I will share Jim's take on Haney's drill with you at the end of this final chapter to emphasize how this type of practice can help improve your swing.

What's so good about getting feedback from Jim McLean is that he is golf's number-one authority on drills, having written two best-selling books on the subject: *Golf Digest's Book of Drills* and *Golf Digest's Ultimate Drill Book*. Besides, Jim believes in his heart and in his head that working on drills is the only honest shortcut to developing a technically sound golf swing, as well as learning to feel and piece together each vital physical key into one flowing motion.

Although Hank Haney is having the biggest influence on Tiger's present golf game, his former teachers all believe in the value of drills and depended on them to help Tiger perfect certain elements of his big swing technique, such as an upright plane and flat left wrist position that are still employed today by Tiger. Smartly, Haney has not toyed with these parts of Tiger's swing machinery, knowing that they are essential to his present movement working as well as it does.

As I learned, drills make practice fun because they allow you to add *purpose* to your sessions on the driving range. When you work on a drill it is for a specific reason— for example, to enhance your balance or smooth out an overly quick tempo.

Tiger has worked hard on drills for most of his entire golfing life. This is because he is experienced enough to know that only through drill work can you learn and groove a brand new swing movement that will change and improve your present action, or correct a serious fault that will enable you to more quickly evolve into a powerful striker of the golf ball. For these reasons particularly, I suggest you work on the following drills, taught to Tiger by his former instructors and, of course, present coach Hank Haney. They are all so simple, they can be explained without photographs.

While speaking to Rudy Duran on the telephone a few years ago, he shared with me an excellent drill he had Tiger work on to improve his balance during the swing. It's essential to be balanced during the swinging action, because only through shifting your weight properly and swinging at the right tempo, with good timing and rhythm, will you be able to bring the club up and down on the correct path and plane and deliver its face solidly into the back of the ball a high percentage of the time.

DURAN'S BALANCE DRILL

On the practice tee, or during a playing lesson on the golf course, Duran had Tiger hit shots and hold the finish position until the ball stopped rolling.

"This drill teaches you to feel and repeat a balanced swing," said Duran.

It's best to start the Balance Drill with a short iron, work up to a medium iron, and then finally a driver. It's also best to try swinging at different speeds, until you find what tempo allows you to stay balanced.

This drill had a good influence on the development of Tiger's game, and there's no doubt it will also help you, provided you are disciplined enough not to "swing out of your shoes" and, instead, "swing within yourself," as Duran and other teachers believe is best.

While working with Tiger's longtime amateur coach John Anselmo on the book *A-Game Golf,* I discovered that he spent hundreds of hours working with Tiger on drills. Anselmo wanted to keep Tiger interested in what he was doing, make the lessons exciting, and teach Tiger the fundamentals of the swing, without talking about complex body positions and superprecise club angles. Anselmo knew, through hard experience, that the more time Tiger devoted to drill practice, the less he would need to concern himself with technique or swing thoughts out on the golf course. Anselmo knew, too, that drills would keep Tiger's swing so polished that when playing in a pressure filled match *feel* would take over. When you play by feel, instead of letting the mind rule your swing action, you are more likely to repeat good mechanics, hit good shots, and keep your cool during a tournament—rather than "choke."

At age ten, when Tiger began taking lessons from Anslemo, he had two main backswing problems: a cupped left wrist and a flat plane. The left wrist is considered cupped when there is an indentation or "cup" between the left hand and left forearm, and this fault causes the club's face to open instead of remaining square. The swing plane is considered flat when the arms move far around the body instead of upward during the backswing, making it difficult to square the club's face to the ball at impact.

ANSELMO'S THUMB-AND-FINGER DRILL

This no-club drill cured Tiger's cupped wrist and flat swing problems. Like Tiger, you'll hit powerfully accurate shots if you employ an upright backswing and keep your left wrist flat at the top, so here's how to practice this drill:

Stand at address with your left arm extended straight down and your palm facing your body. Grasp your left thumb with your right hand. Gently pull your left arm back as far as is comfortably possible and then freeze the backswing position for ten seconds. Immediately, you'll feel how upright your swing is and that you've achieved the ideal, flat left wrist position.

Although Tiger won eight major championships under Butch Harmon, when he first started taking lessons from Butch in 1993 he had problems timing his driver swing and often hit off-line shots. In addition, he could not control his distance when playing full wedge shots into a green. The fault that was causing both these problems was not coordinating the sequencing movements of the body and club, so the following drill was prescribed.

HARMON'S SLOW-MOTION SWING DRILL

Concentrate on swinging at 75 percent of your full-out speed. This drill forces you to use the big muscles in your back, arms, and shoulders, rather than the small muscles in your hands and wrists that prevent you from swinging smoothly. It will also force you to use fluid footwork to put rhythm into your action, which is precisely why Harmon believes that "the swing starts from the ground up."

Repeat this drill until the swinging action feels effortless. That sensation will tell you that the elements of timing and rhythm governing your body and club motions are in sync. Now keep increasing your speed until you find the ideal tempo that allows you to stay in control and hit the strongest and straightest shots.

The practicing of drills is as important to playing good golf as exercise is to keeping your blood pressure at a healthy level. Furthermore, the type of drill a teacher recommends a student work on usually relates to the player's swing problem and reflects the teacher's swing philosophy. On that note, it seems Haney's views of swing technique have not changed all that much since 1991, when I spoke to him and ranked him among *Golf Magazine*'s top 50 best teachers in America.

Before getting into Haney's drill, I want to point out how easy it is to slip up and hurt your swing by practicing something that is not suited to your game.

Prior to taking formal lessons from Haney, Tiger was spotted practicing a baseball swing drill that involves holding the club a couple of feet off the ground, and from that starting position swinging back and through. Well, Haney also teaches O'Meara, and this drill surely has proven itself to help O'Meara swing on a desired flat plane, hit the ball well, and win major championships. However, for a guy like Tiger, who performs better swinging on an upright angle, this drill was the last drill he should have been working on.

Fortunately, Hank Haney came to the rescue, recommending a drill specifically suited to Tiger's swing needs, which is a mark of an excellent teacher. Your lesson: Only work on drills suited to your game. That said, the drills recommended thus far, and the one of Haney's that follows, are for very common problems. Still, check with your local golf professional to make sure the drills you choose to work on are designed to help you groove a desired new move your teacher prefers you learn or correct a swing problem your teacher confirms you really and truly have.

When McLean saw Haney teaching Tiger in early 2003, it's apparent Tiger's coach had a specific purpose in mind—I believe it was to get Tiger accustomed to swinging the club out, then in, then up and around the body, as the shoulders rotate clockwise.

The photographs contained in this book, particularly those contained in the color insert, prove that Tiger is now swinging the club on a pure plane, and "hitting the ball beautifully," as Tiger himself admitted in June, after the 2005 U.S. Open and, once again, after winning the British Open that July. Moreover, his big wins at Doral and the Masters earlier in the year prove Haney's drill helped Tiger get back on track—on the practice tee and on the golf course. This is something I believe he will be doing for a long time to come and, hopefully, so will you.

HANEY'S NO-CLUB DRILL

Pick a target. Take your address, extending your left arm straight down, such that your palm faces you and an imaginary line running horizontally across your knuckles is parallel to the target line.

Next, grasp your left wrist with your right hand. Next, push your left hand and left arm outward. Next, rotate your shoulders clockwise until your left arm parallels the target line. Last, swing the arms upward.

Since Tiger's new swing is based on what he learned from four professional teachers—not just Hank Haney—work on all the drills presented in this chapter. Each and every practice drill will serve as a building block in your quest to become a technically sound swinger of the golf club and to hit solid, accurate shots, particularly off the tee.

AFTERWORD

O n Sunday, July 17, 2005, Tiger Woods raised his already great game to an even higher level to win the coveted claret jug that is given to the winner of what Americans call the British Open and golf aficionados overseas refer to as The Open Championship.

On that beautiful Scottish evening at St. Andrews, the home of golf, Tiger was also crowned the "champion golfer of the year" as he was given the gold medal presented to all champions.

This was a historic championship, because ironically two days earlier, after narrowly missing the cut, Jack Nicklaus—Tiger's idol and the golfer who holds the record of eighteen major championships—waved good-bye to fans from all over the world and wiped tears from his eyes as he walked off the eighteenth green. Nicklaus will never again compete in the British Open, but there can be no more talented and humble a golfer to take his place at the top than Tiger Woods, who after winning his tenth major by five strokes came closer to matching Nicklaus's major championship record.

Tiger's goal is to break Nicklaus's major championship record, and judging from his most recent near-flawless performance, he eventually will. I'm confident in saying this because of how well Tiger's new swing stood up under pressure and allowed him to hit powerfully accurate drives and take control of the championship. There is no question that Tiger's swing is now more technically sound than ever before. In fact, after Tiger won the British Open and joined Jack Nicklaus as the only golfer ever to have won all four major championships twice, Nicklaus commented that he had never seen Tiger swing so well. From such a heroic figure, there can be no better endorsement.

Tiger's wins at the British Open and at the Masters in 2005 should be an inspiration to all golfers, no matter what their handicap. Tiger is living proof that if you work hard to make changes to your swing and follow the guidelines put forth in the book you have just read, you too can become a better player. As good as Tiger was, he strived to improve and he succeeded, largely with the help of his new coach, Hank Haney, but also through constructive practice.

Your lesson: Whether your schedule allows you to visit the driving range every day or only for an hour a week, practice with a purpose and follow a well-thought-out plan that includes setting personal goals. Don't simply "beat balls." Instead, work on new swing positions and ingrain them into your muscle memory through drills, and always aim at a specific target. Furthermore, find a tempo of swing that allows you to hit the ball solidly and in the fairway, for, as even Tiger learned, distance off the tee is only a good thing if you combine it with accuracy. The reason is that hitting fairways is the first step to putting the ball in a position that allows you to hit an attacking approach shot and shoot low scores.

INDEX

Note: Page numbers in italics indicate photographs and art.

Author **JOHN ANDRISANI** is the former senior editor of instruction at *Golf Magazine*. A former golf instructor, Andrisani is the author of over twenty-five books, including the best-selling *The Tiger Woods Way*. He has also written books with golf's top tour players, such as John Daly and Fred Couples, as well as top-ranked teachers, most notably two of Tiger Woods's former instructors, John Anselmo and Butch Harmon.

A course record holder and past winner of the World Golf Writers' Championship, Andrisani resides in Gulfport, Florida.

Photographer **YASUHIRO TANABE** does work for top golf magazines around the world, and his photographs have appeared in such books as the best-selling *The Plane Truth for Golfers,* by Jim Hardy with John Andrisani.

ALLEN WELKIS is an award-winning illustrator whose work has appeared in *Golf Magazine* and in several golf books, including *The Tiger Woods Way* and *The Short Game Magic of Tiger Woods*.